Virtual Vogue

Fashioning Futuristic Avatars

Written by

Dominique Devereaux

MetaEditor-in-Chief

MetaCouture

Artwork by

MetaCOUTURE
MetaCouture

Credits

Written: January 4, 2024

Written by

Dominique Devereaux

MetaEditor-in-Chief

MetaCouture

Artwork by

MetaCouture 2024

This book was written in association with MetaCouture by and with RuPaul Getty, the world's first transgender MetaReporter and Style MetaReporter of MetaCouture and in association with some AI elements.

Overview

"Virtual Vogue: Fashioning Futuristic Avatars" is a comprehensive guide that explores the exciting world of virtual fashion design. This book delves into the evolution of fashion and the rise of virtual fashion, highlighting the advantages and challenges in this innovative field. Readers will learn how to create and customize avatars, understand virtual body measurements, and personalize their virtual fashion experience. The book also covers the art of couture and how to adapt it for avatars, including virtual fabric selection, couture techniques, and fashion shows. Additionally, it delves into the intersection of virtual fashion and technology, marketing, sustainability, and entertainment, providing valuable insights into the future of this industry. Whether you're a fashion enthusiast, designer, or simply curious about the future of fashion, "Virtual Vogue" is must-read.

Contents

1 Introduction to Virtual Fashion

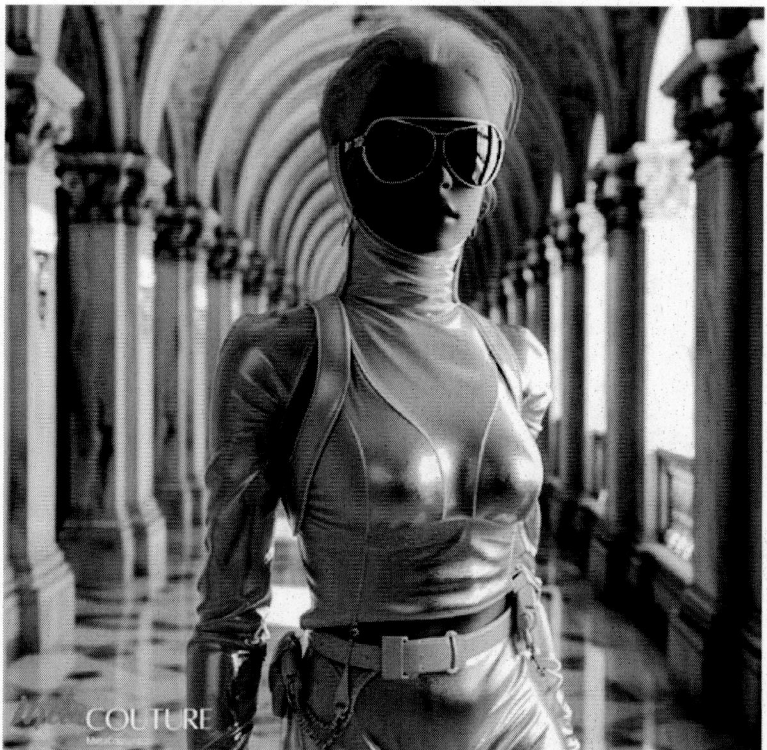

1.1 The Evolution of Fashion

Fashion has always been a reflection of society, culture, and individual expression. Throughout history, fashion has evolved and transformed, adapting to the changing times and trends. From the ancient civilizations to the modern era, fashion has played a significant role in shaping our identities and how we present ourselves to the world.

1.1.1 Early Beginnings

The origins of fashion can be traced back to ancient civilizations such as Egypt, Greece, and Rome. In these early societies, clothing was not only a practical necessity but also a symbol of social status and wealth. The wealthy elites would adorn themselves in luxurious fabrics and intricate designs, while the common people would wear simpler garments made from more affordable materials.

As time went on, fashion began to evolve and become more accessible to the masses. The Middle Ages saw the rise of guilds and trade associations, which led to the development of specialized skills in textile production and garment making. This period also marked the emergence of fashion trends and the concept of "style," as people started to experiment with different silhouettes and embellishments.

1.1.2 The Renaissance and Beyond

The Renaissance period brought about a significant shift in fashion. It was a time of great artistic and cultural revival, and fashion became a means of self-expression and individuality. The invention of the printing press allowed for the dissemination of fashion ideas and trends, leading to the rise of fashion magazines and the spread of fashion knowledge.

During the 18th and 19th centuries, fashion became closely tied to social and political movements. The French Revolution, for example, brought about a radical change in fashion, as the aristocracy's extravagant styles were replaced by more modest and practical clothing. The Industrial Revolution further revolutionized the fashion industry, with the introduction of mass production techniques and the availability of ready-to-wear clothing.

1.1.3 The Birth of Haute Couture

In the mid-19th century, the concept of haute couture emerged in Paris, France. Haute couture, meaning "high sewing" in French, referred to the creation of custom-made garments for individual clients. This marked a shift towards more exclusive and luxurious fashion, with designers like Charles Frederick Worth and Paul Poiret leading the way.

Haute couture became synonymous with craftsmanship, attention to detail, and exquisite design. It was a celebration of creativity and artistry, with designers pushing the boundaries of fashion and creating one-of-a-kind pieces. The couture houses became the epitome of luxury and elegance, attracting clients from around the world.

1.1.4 The Rise of Ready-to-Wear

While haute couture continued to thrive, the 20th century saw the rise of ready-to-wear fashion. With the advent of industrialization and mass production, clothing became more affordable and accessible to a wider audience. Ready-to-wear collections offered fashionable clothing at a fraction of the cost of couture, allowing people from all walks of life to participate in the latest trends.

The fashion industry continued to evolve with the introduction of new materials, technologies, and design techniques. The 1960s and 1970s witnessed a revolution in fashion, with designers like Mary Quant and Yves Saint Laurent challenging traditional norms and embracing a more youthful and rebellious aesthetic. The rise of street style and subcultures further diversified the fashion landscape, giving rise to new trends and styles.

1.1.5 The Digital Age and Virtual Fashion

In recent years, the fashion industry has been undergoing another transformation with the advent of virtual fashion. Virtual fashion refers to the creation of digital garments and accessories that can be worn by avatars in virtual environments. It combines the worlds of fashion and technology, offering new possibilities for creativity, sustainability, and personal expression.

Virtual fashion allows designers to experiment with unconventional materials, shapes, and colors that may not be feasible in the physical world. It offers a platform for self-expression and individuality, where people can create their unique style without the limitations of physical constraints. Virtual fashion also opens up new avenues for collaboration and global connectivity, as designers and consumers can interact and share their creations in virtual spaces.

1.1.6 The Future of Fashion

As we look to the future, it is clear that virtual fashion will continue to play a significant role in the fashion industry. With advancements in technology such as virtual reality and augmented reality, the boundaries between the physical and virtual worlds will continue to blur. Virtual fashion shows, virtual showrooms, and virtual try-on experiences will become more commonplace, allowing consumers to engage with fashion in new and exciting ways.

However, the rise of virtual fashion also presents challenges and considerations. Designers will need to adapt their skills and embrace new technologies to stay relevant in a rapidly changing industry. Collaboration and interdisciplinary approaches will become increasingly important, as fashion designers work alongside technologists, 3D artists, and virtual reality experts.

In conclusion, the evolution of fashion has been a journey of creativity, innovation, and self-expression. From the ancient civilizations to the digital age, fashion has continuously adapted to the changing times and embraced new possibilities. Virtual fashion represents the next frontier, offering limitless opportunities for designers and consumers alike. By understanding the evolution of fashion and preparing for the future, we can embrace virtual fashion as a powerful tool for self-expression and creativity.

1.2 The Rise of Virtual Fashion

In recent years, the fashion industry has witnessed a significant shift towards virtual fashion. With the rise of technology and the increasing popularity of virtual reality (VR) and augmented reality (AR), fashion designers are exploring new avenues to create innovative and futuristic designs for avatars. This chapter delves into the rise of virtual fashion, its advantages, and the challenges faced by designers in this emerging field.

1.2.1 The Emergence of Virtual Fashion

Virtual fashion refers to the creation of digital garments and accessories that can be worn by avatars in virtual environments. It allows individuals to express their personal style and experiment with fashion without the limitations of physical clothing. The concept of virtual fashion has gained traction in recent years due to advancements in technology and the growing interest in virtual experiences.

The emergence of virtual fashion can be attributed to several factors. Firstly, the increasing popularity of virtual reality has opened up new possibilities for fashion designers. VR technology allows users to immerse themselves in virtual worlds, where they can interact with digital objects and characters. This has created a demand for virtual clothing that can enhance the user's virtual experience and allow them to express their individuality.

Secondly, the rise of social media and online gaming has contributed to the growth of virtual fashion. Platforms like

Instagram and TikTok have become popular spaces for individuals to showcase their virtual fashion creations. Online games, such as Second Life and Fortnite, have also created virtual economies where players can buy and sell virtual clothing items. This has created a market for virtual fashion designers and has given rise to a new form of digital self-expression.

1.2.2 Advantages of Virtual Fashion

Virtual fashion offers several advantages over traditional fashion design. Firstly, it provides designers with unlimited creative possibilities. In the virtual realm, designers are not constrained by the limitations of physical materials and can experiment with unconventional shapes, textures, and colors. This allows for the creation of avant-garde and boundary-pushing designs that may not be feasible in the physical world.

Secondly, virtual fashion offers a sustainable alternative to traditional fashion. The fashion industry is known for its negative environmental impact, with the production and disposal of clothing contributing to pollution and waste. Virtual fashion eliminates the need for physical production, reducing the industry's carbon footprint. Additionally, virtual garments can be easily shared and reused, promoting a more circular and sustainable fashion economy.

Furthermore, virtual fashion provides a platform for inclusivity and diversity. Avatars can be customized to represent individuals of all shapes, sizes, and backgrounds. This allows for the creation of fashion that is inclusive and representative of a diverse range of identities. Virtual fashion also offers the opportunity for individuals to experiment with different styles and personas, empowering them to express themselves authentically.

1.2.3 Challenges in Virtual Fashion Design

While virtual fashion presents exciting opportunities, it also comes with its own set of challenges for designers. One of the main challenges is the technical aspect of creating virtual garments. Designers need to have a strong understanding of 3D modeling and simulation techniques to bring their designs to life. They must also consider factors such as virtual body measurements and movement to ensure that the garments fit and behave realistically on avatars.

Another challenge is the lack of tactile experience in virtual fashion. In traditional fashion design, designers can touch and feel fabrics, allowing them to make informed decisions about materials and textures. In virtual fashion, designers rely on visual cues and simulations to determine the look and feel of garments. This requires a different skill set and a keen eye for detail.

Additionally, virtual fashion designers need to consider the user experience and functionality of their designs. Virtual garments should not only look visually appealing but also enhance the user's virtual experience. Designers must consider factors such as ease of movement, comfort, and interaction with other virtual objects.

Furthermore, the virtual fashion industry is still in its early stages, and there is a lack of established standards and best practices. Designers need to navigate this evolving landscape and stay updated with the latest technologies and trends. Collaboration and knowledge-sharing within the virtual fashion community are crucial for overcoming these challenges and pushing the boundaries of virtual fashion design.

In the next chapter, we will explore the process of creating avatars and the customization options available to designers. We will delve into the intricacies of virtual body measurements and the importance of avatar personalization in virtual fashion design.

1.3 Advantages of Virtual Fashion

Virtual fashion, the art of designing and creating clothing for avatars in virtual environments, offers numerous advantages that are revolutionizing the fashion industry. As technology continues to advance, virtual fashion is becoming increasingly popular and is poised to shape the future of the industry. In this section, we will explore the advantages of virtual fashion and how it is transforming the way we think about clothing design and consumption.

1.3.1 Unlimited Creativity and Experimentation

One of the most significant advantages of virtual fashion is the freedom it provides for designers to unleash their creativity and experiment with innovative designs. Unlike traditional fashion, where physical limitations and production costs can restrict creativity, virtual fashion allows designers to push boundaries and explore new possibilities. With virtual tools and software, designers can create garments that defy gravity, manipulate fabrics in ways that are impossible in the physical world, and experiment with unconventional shapes and structures. This unlimited creative freedom opens up a whole new realm of possibilities for fashion designers, enabling them to create truly unique and groundbreaking designs.

1.3.2 Cost and Time Efficiency

Virtual fashion offers significant cost and time savings compared to traditional fashion design and production processes. In the physical world, creating a garment from scratch involves numerous steps, including sourcing materials, pattern making, sample production, and fitting sessions. These processes can be time-consuming and expensive. In contrast, virtual fashion allows designers to skip many of these steps by creating and visualizing garments digitally. With virtual tools, designers can quickly prototype and iterate designs, eliminating the need for physical samples and reducing production costs. Additionally, virtual fashion enables designers to showcase their creations in virtual fashion shows, eliminating the need for physical runway shows, which can be costly and logistically challenging.

1.3.3 Sustainable and Ethical Fashion

Virtual fashion has the potential to address some of the sustainability and ethical challenges faced by the traditional fashion industry. The production of physical garments often involves the use of scarce resources, excessive waste generation, and unethical labor practices. Virtual fashion, on the other hand, offers a more sustainable and ethical alternative. By designing and showcasing clothing digitally, virtual fashion reduces the need for physical production, minimizing the environmental impact associated with traditional fashion. Additionally, virtual fashion allows for the exploration of alternative materials and fabrication techniques that are more sustainable and eco-friendly. Furthermore, virtual fashion can promote ethical practices by eliminating the need for sweatshops and exploitative labor conditions.

1.3.4 Accessibility and Inclusivity

Virtual fashion has the potential to make fashion more accessible and inclusive. In the physical world, fashion is often limited by size, shape, and physical abilities. Virtual fashion, however, transcends these limitations by allowing users to create and customize avatars that represent their ideal selves. Virtual fashion enables individuals of all body types, sizes, and abilities to express their personal style and experiment with different looks. It also provides a platform for underrepresented communities to showcase their unique fashion perspectives and challenge traditional beauty standards. By embracing virtual fashion, the industry can become more inclusive and celebrate diversity in all its forms.

1.3.5 Global Reach and Collaboration

Virtual fashion has the power to connect designers, consumers, and industry professionals from around the world. Through virtual platforms and social media, designers can showcase their creations to a global audience, breaking down geographical barriers and reaching a wider customer base. Virtual fashion also facilitates collaboration between designers, allowing them to work together on projects regardless of their physical location. This global reach and collaboration foster creativity, innovation, and cultural exchange, enriching the fashion industry as a whole.

1.3.6 Enhanced Shopping Experience

Virtual fashion offers an enhanced shopping experience for consumers. With virtual reality and augmented reality technologies, shoppers can virtually try on garments, experiment with different styles and colors, and visualize how the clothing will look on their avatars. This immersive and interactive shopping experience allows consumers to make more informed purchasing decisions and reduces the likelihood of returns. Virtual fashion also enables personalized recommendations and styling advice based on individual preferences and body measurements, enhancing the overall shopping experience and customer satisfaction.

In conclusion, virtual fashion brings numerous advantages to the fashion industry. From unlimited creativity and experimentation to cost and time efficiency, sustainability, accessibility, global reach, and enhanced shopping experiences, virtual fashion is transforming the way we design, create, and consume fashion. As the industry continues to evolve, embracing virtual fashion will be crucial for designers and fashion professionals to stay relevant and prepare for the future of fashion.

1.4 Challenges in Virtual Fashion Design

Designing virtual fashion for avatars presents a unique set of challenges that designers must navigate in order to create stunning and realistic virtual couture. While the virtual fashion industry offers exciting opportunities for creativity and innovation, it also comes with its own set of obstacles. In this section, we will explore some of the key challenges that designers face in virtual fashion design and how they can overcome them.

1.4.1 Creating Realistic Avatars

One of the primary challenges in virtual fashion design is creating avatars that accurately represent the human body. Avatars serve as the canvas for virtual couture, and it is crucial for designers to ensure that they are realistic and proportionate. However, achieving this level of realism can be difficult, as avatars come in various shapes, sizes, and proportions. Designers must invest time and effort in understanding virtual body measurements and customization techniques to create avatars that accurately reflect the diversity of human bodies.

1.4.2 Virtual Fabric Simulation

Another significant challenge in virtual fashion design is simulating the behavior of fabrics in the virtual environment. Real fabrics have unique characteristics such as drape, texture, and movement, which greatly influence the overall look and feel of a garment. Replicating these characteristics in the virtual world requires advanced simulation techniques and accurate physics models. Designers must invest in software and tools that can accurately simulate fabric behavior to ensure that their virtual couture looks and behaves realistically.

1.4.3 Technical Constraints

Virtual fashion design also comes with technical constraints that designers must consider. The software and tools used for virtual fashion design may have limitations in terms of rendering capabilities, polygon counts, and file formats. These constraints can impact the complexity and level of detail that designers can achieve in their virtual couture. It is essential for designers to understand the technical limitations of the platforms they are working with and find creative solutions to work within those constraints.

1.4.4 Collaboration and Communication

Collaboration and communication are crucial aspects of fashion design, and virtual fashion is no exception. However, working in a virtual environment can pose challenges in terms of effective collaboration and communication between designers, developers, and other stakeholders. Designers must find ways to effectively communicate their ideas, provide feedback, and collaborate with others remotely. Utilizing virtual collaboration tools, video conferencing, and clear communication channels can help overcome these challenges and ensure smooth collaboration in virtual fashion design.

1.4.5 Intellectual Property and Copyright

Virtual fashion design raises important questions regarding intellectual property and copyright. As virtual fashion becomes more prevalent, designers must navigate the legal implications of creating and distributing virtual couture. Protecting original designs, preventing unauthorized copying, and understanding the legal framework surrounding virtual fashion are essential for designers to safeguard their work and ensure fair compensation for their creativity.

1.4.6 User Experience and Interactivity

Virtual fashion design offers the opportunity to create interactive and immersive experiences for users. However, designing for user experience in the virtual world requires a different approach compared to traditional fashion design. Designers must consider how users will interact with virtual garments, how they will customize and personalize their avatars, and how the virtual fashion will integrate with other virtual environments or platforms. Creating a seamless and engaging user experience is a challenge that designers must address to ensure the success of their virtual fashion creations.

1.4.7 Keeping Up with Technological Advancements

The virtual fashion industry is constantly evolving, with new technologies and tools emerging regularly. Designers must stay updated with the latest advancements in virtual reality, augmented reality, 3D modeling, and simulation to remain competitive in the field. Keeping up with these technological advancements can be a challenge, as it requires continuous learning and adaptation. However, embracing new technologies can also open up new possibilities and expand the creative potential of virtual fashion design.

In conclusion, virtual fashion design presents a range of challenges that designers must overcome to create stunning and realistic virtual couture. From creating realistic avatars to simulating fabric behavior and navigating technical constraints, designers must be prepared to tackle these obstacles. Effective collaboration, understanding legal implications, designing for user experience, and staying updated with technological advancements are all essential for success in the virtual fashion industry. By embracing these challenges and finding innovative solutions, designers can shape the future of virtual fashion and create truly transformative experiences for fashion enthusiasts in the digital realm.

2 Creating Avatars

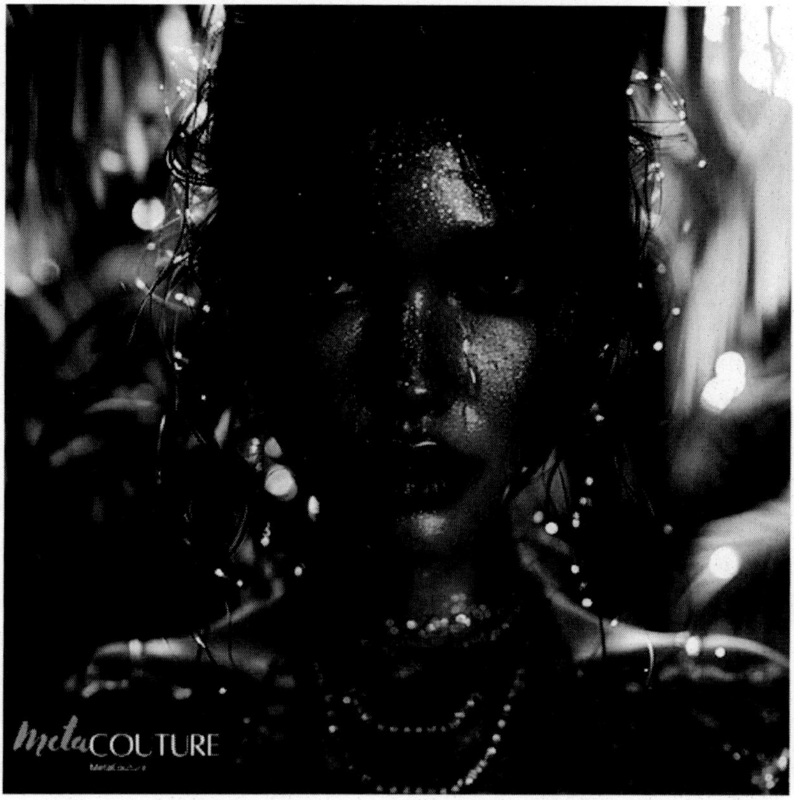

2.1 Understanding Avatars

Avatars have become an integral part of the virtual fashion industry, allowing individuals to express their personal style and creativity in a digital realm. In this chapter, we will delve into the world of avatars, exploring their significance, characteristics, and the role they play in virtual fashion design.

2.1.1 The Definition of Avatars

Avatars, in the context of virtual fashion, refer to digital representations of individuals that can be customized and styled according to their preferences. These virtual beings serve as the canvas for fashion designers to showcase their creations and allow users to experiment with different looks and styles. Avatars can range from realistic human-like figures to fantastical creatures, depending on the virtual environment and purpose.

2.1.2 The Importance of Avatars in Virtual Fashion

Avatars are the key element that bridges the gap between the physical and virtual worlds of fashion. They provide a platform for designers to showcase their creations and allow users to experience the joy of dressing up and expressing themselves in a virtual setting. Avatars enable individuals to explore different fashion styles, experiment with trends, and push the boundaries of traditional fashion.

Moreover, avatars offer a unique opportunity for inclusivity and representation in the fashion industry. They allow individuals to create digital versions of themselves that may differ from their physical appearance, providing a space for self-expression and identity exploration. Avatars can transcend societal norms and limitations, empowering individuals to embrace their true selves without fear of judgment or discrimination.

2.1.3 The Anatomy of Avatars

To effectively design couture fashion for avatars, it is crucial to understand their anatomy and structure. Avatars typically consist of various components, including the head, body, limbs, and accessories. Each component can be customized and modified to create a unique and personalized avatar.

The head of an avatar encompasses facial features such as eyes, nose, mouth, and hair. Designers can experiment with different hairstyles, facial expressions, and makeup options to enhance the overall look and feel of the avatar. The body of an avatar includes the torso, arms, and legs, which can be adjusted in terms of size, shape, and proportions. This flexibility allows designers to cater to a diverse range of body types and sizes, promoting body positivity and inclusivity.

In addition to the basic components, avatars can be adorned with various accessories such as jewelry, hats, shoes, and bags. These accessories add an extra layer of personalization and style to the avatar, allowing users to create unique and eye-catching looks.

2.1.4 Avatar Customization Tools

To facilitate avatar customization, virtual fashion platforms provide users with a range of tools and options. These tools allow users to modify various aspects of their avatars, including body shape, skin tone, facial features, and clothing. Users can experiment with different combinations and styles, creating a virtual representation that aligns with their personal taste and fashion preferences.

Some platforms offer advanced customization features, such as the ability to adjust body proportions, muscle definition, and even facial expressions. These tools enable users to create avatars that closely resemble their physical appearance or embody their desired fantasy persona.

2.1.5 The Role of Technology in Avatar Creation

Advancements in technology have played a significant role in enhancing the realism and customization options of avatars. 3D modeling and scanning techniques allow for more accurate representations of individuals, capturing intricate details and nuances of their physical appearance. This level of realism enables designers to create couture fashion that seamlessly integrates with the avatar's body, enhancing the overall visual experience.

Furthermore, virtual reality (VR) and augmented reality (AR) technologies have revolutionized the way avatars are created and experienced. VR allows users to immerse themselves in a virtual environment, interacting with their avatars in a more immersive and realistic manner. AR, on the other hand, overlays virtual elements onto the real world, enabling users to see and interact with their avatars in their physical surroundings. These technologies open up new possibilities for fashion designers to showcase their creations and for users to engage with virtual fashion in a more interactive and engaging way.

In conclusion, avatars are the foundation of virtual fashion design, providing a platform for creativity, self-expression, and inclusivity. Understanding the anatomy and customization options of avatars is essential for designers to create couture fashion that seamlessly integrates with the virtual world. With advancements in technology, the future of avatar creation holds even more exciting possibilities, pushing the boundaries of virtual fashion and revolutionizing the way we perceive and engage with fashion.

2.2 Avatar Customization

Avatar customization is a crucial aspect of virtual fashion design. It allows individuals to express their unique style and personality through their digital representations. In this section, we will explore the various elements of avatar customization and how designers can create a personalized and immersive experience for their users.

2.2.1 Understanding Avatar Customization

Avatar customization refers to the process of modifying the appearance of a virtual character or avatar. It involves selecting and adjusting various attributes such as facial features, body shape, skin tone, hair style, and clothing. The goal is to create a digital representation that closely resembles the user's desired look and style.

Designers must understand the importance of avatar customization in virtual fashion. It is not just about creating a visually appealing avatar but also about providing a sense of identity and self-expression to the users. By allowing users to customize their avatars, designers empower them to become active participants in the virtual fashion world.

2.2.2 Customization Options

To create a comprehensive avatar customization system, designers need to offer a wide range of options for users to choose from. These options can include:

2.2.2.1 Facial Features

Users should have the ability to modify facial features such as eye shape, nose shape, mouth shape, and skin tone. This allows them to create avatars that resemble their real-life appearance or experiment with different looks.

2.2.2.2 Body Shape

The ability to customize body shape is essential in virtual fashion design. Users should be able to adjust parameters such as height, weight, body proportions, and muscle definition. This allows for a diverse range of avatars that cater to different body types and sizes.

2.2.2.3 Hair Style

Hair style plays a significant role in personal expression. Designers should provide a variety of hair options, including length, color, texture, and style. This allows users to create avatars with hairstyles that reflect their individuality.

2.2.2.4 Clothing and Accessories

Virtual fashion is incomplete without the ability to customize clothing and accessories. Designers should offer a wide range of options, including different styles, colors, patterns, and materials. Users should be able to mix and match various clothing items to create unique outfits.

2.2.3 Personalization and Realism

To enhance the user experience, designers should strive for personalization and realism in avatar customization. This can be achieved through the following techniques:

2.2.3.1 Realistic Textures and Materials

Using high-quality textures and materials can significantly enhance the realism of virtual fashion. Designers should pay attention to details such as fabric textures, stitching, and draping. By accurately replicating real-world materials, users can have a more immersive and authentic experience.

2.2.3.2 Animation and Movement

Incorporating realistic animation and movement into avatars adds another layer of personalization. Designers should consider how clothing and accessories interact with the avatar's body during different movements. This attention to detail creates a more lifelike and dynamic virtual fashion experience.

2.2.3.3 User Feedback and Iteration

To ensure user satisfaction, designers should gather feedback from users and iterate on the customization options. This can be done through surveys, focus groups, or user testing sessions. By actively involving users in the design process, designers can create a more user-centric avatar customization system.

2.2.4 Challenges in Avatar Customization

While avatar customization offers immense creative possibilities, designers also face certain challenges in this process. Some of the common challenges include:

2.2.4.1 Technical Limitations

Designing a robust avatar customization system requires advanced technical capabilities. Designers need to consider factors such as rendering capabilities, file size limitations, and compatibility across different platforms. Overcoming these technical limitations can be a complex task.

2.2.4.2 Balancing Complexity and Simplicity

Offering a wide range of customization options can be overwhelming for users. Designers need to strike a balance between providing enough options for personalization and keeping the interface intuitive and user-friendly. Simplifying the customization process without compromising on creativity is a challenge that designers must address.

2.2.4.3 Cultural Sensitivity

Designers must be mindful of cultural sensitivities when designing avatar customization options. Different cultures have unique beauty standards and fashion preferences. It is essential to offer a diverse range of options that cater to various cultural backgrounds and avoid perpetuating stereotypes or biases.

Conclusion

Avatar customization is a vital aspect of virtual fashion design. By offering a wide range of customization options and prioritizing personalization and realism, designers can create a more immersive and engaging experience for users. However, they must also navigate challenges such as technical limitations, balancing complexity and simplicity, and cultural sensitivity. By addressing these challenges, designers can create a future where virtual fashion and avatar customization go hand in hand, allowing individuals to express their unique style and creativity.

2.3 Virtual Body Measurements

In the world of virtual fashion, one of the key aspects of creating realistic and visually appealing avatars is ensuring accurate virtual body measurements. Just like in the physical world, where designers take precise measurements of models to create well-fitting garments, virtual fashion designers must also consider the unique body proportions and measurements of avatars.

2.3.1 Understanding Avatar Proportions

Avatars come in various shapes and sizes, and it is essential for virtual fashion designers to understand the different proportions that avatars can have. While some avatars may have realistic human proportions, others may have exaggerated features or non-human characteristics. Understanding these proportions is crucial for creating garments that fit well and enhance the avatar's appearance.

Virtual fashion designers must consider factors such as the length of the avatar's limbs, the size of their head, the width of their shoulders, and the overall body shape. By studying these proportions, designers can ensure that their creations are visually appealing and well-suited to the avatar's unique physique.

2.3.2 Capturing Virtual Body Measurements

To create garments that fit perfectly on avatars, virtual fashion designers need to capture accurate virtual body measurements. This process involves using advanced technologies such as 3D scanning or motion capture to obtain precise data about the avatar's body shape and size.

One common method for capturing virtual body measurements is through the use of 3D scanning. This technology allows designers to create a digital representation of the avatar's body by scanning it from multiple angles. The resulting 3D model provides designers with detailed measurements that can be used to create garments that fit the avatar's body shape accurately.

Another method is motion capture, which involves tracking the movements of a real-life model and transferring them to the avatar. By capturing the model's body movements, designers can obtain valuable information about the avatar's body proportions and how garments should move and drape on the virtual body.

2.3.3 Customizing Virtual Body Measurements

In addition to capturing accurate virtual body measurements, virtual fashion designers also need to provide customization options for avatars. Just as people have different body shapes and sizes in the physical world, avatars should have the ability to adjust their measurements to reflect their individual preferences.

Virtual fashion platforms often provide tools that allow users to modify their avatar's body measurements. These tools enable users to adjust parameters such as height, weight, body proportions, and even specific body parts like waist size or shoulder width. By offering customization options, designers can ensure that their garments fit a wide range of avatar body types and cater to individual preferences.

2.3.4 Challenges in Virtual Body Measurements

While capturing and customizing virtual body measurements is essential for creating realistic and well-fitting garments, there are several challenges that virtual fashion designers may face in this process.

One challenge is the diversity of avatar body types. Avatars can have a wide range of body shapes and sizes, including non-human or fantastical proportions. Designers must consider these variations and create garments that can adapt to different body types while still maintaining their intended aesthetic.

Another challenge is the limitations of current technology. While 3D scanning and motion capture have advanced significantly, there may still be limitations in accurately capturing certain body features or movements. Designers must work within these limitations and find creative solutions to ensure that their garments fit well on avatars.

Additionally, the customization options provided to users may vary depending on the virtual fashion platform. Designers must consider the limitations of these customization tools and find ways to create garments that can be adjusted to fit a wide range of body measurements.

2.3.5 The Future of Virtual Body Measurements

As technology continues to advance, the future of virtual body measurements holds exciting possibilities for virtual fashion designers. Here are some potential developments that may shape the future of this field:

2.3.5.1 Advanced Scanning and Simulation Techniques

Advancements in scanning and simulation technologies may allow for even more accurate and detailed virtual body measurements. High-resolution 3D scanning techniques could capture finer details of the avatar's body, resulting in garments that fit even more precisely. Additionally, simulation techniques could enable designers to predict how garments will move and drape on avatars with greater accuracy.

2.3.5.2 Artificial Intelligence and Machine Learning

Artificial intelligence and machine learning algorithms could play a significant role in virtual body measurements. These technologies could analyze vast amounts of data to identify patterns and correlations between body measurements and garment fit. By leveraging this knowledge, designers could create garments that automatically adapt to different avatar body types, reducing the need for manual customization.

2.3.5.3 Virtual Try-On Experiences

Virtual try-on experiences could become more immersive and realistic, allowing users to see how garments fit and move on their avatars in real-time. By combining virtual reality or augmented reality technologies with accurate virtual body measurements, users could virtually try on garments and make adjustments to achieve the perfect fit before making a purchase.

2.3.5.4 Collaboration and User Feedback

Collaboration between virtual fashion designers and users could play a crucial role in improving virtual body measurements. By actively involving users in the design process and gathering feedback on garment fit and customization options, designers can continuously refine their virtual body measurement techniques and create garments that better meet the needs and preferences of users.

In conclusion, virtual body measurements are a vital aspect of creating realistic and well-fitting garments for avatars in the world of virtual fashion. By understanding avatar proportions, capturing accurate measurements, providing customization options, and addressing the challenges in this process, virtual fashion designers can create garments that enhance the virtual fashion experience. With advancements in technology and the potential for AI, virtual try-on experiences, and collaboration, the future of virtual body measurements holds exciting possibilities for the virtual fashion industry.

2.4 Avatar Personalization

In the world of virtual fashion, one of the most exciting aspects is the ability to personalize avatars. Avatar personalization allows individuals to express their unique style and personality through their virtual representation. It is a key element in creating a truly immersive and engaging virtual fashion experience. In this section, we will explore the importance of avatar personalization and discuss various techniques and tools that can be used to achieve it.

2.4.1 Understanding the Importance of Avatar Personalization

Avatar personalization plays a crucial role in virtual fashion as it allows users to create a digital representation of themselves that reflects their individuality. Just like in the real world, people have different body types, skin tones, and personal preferences when it comes to fashion. By offering a wide range of customization options, virtual fashion designers can cater to the diverse needs and desires of their users.

Personalization also enhances the sense of ownership and connection that users feel towards their avatars. When individuals can create avatars that resemble themselves or embody their desired image, they are more likely to engage with virtual fashion experiences and invest in virtual clothing and accessories. This sense of ownership can lead to increased user satisfaction and loyalty.

2.4.2 Techniques for Avatar Personalization

There are several techniques that virtual fashion designers can employ to enable avatar personalization. Let's explore some of the most common ones:

2.4.2.1 Avatar Customization Options

Providing a wide range of customization options is essential for avatar personalization. This includes allowing users to modify their avatar's facial features, body shape, hair style, and clothing. Designers can offer sliders, color pickers, and other interactive tools to enable users to fine-tune their avatars to their liking. By offering a diverse set of options, designers can ensure that users can create avatars that truly represent their unique identity.

2.4.2.2 Virtual Wardrobe

Another effective technique for avatar personalization is the inclusion of a virtual wardrobe. This feature allows users to select and change their avatar's clothing and accessories. Designers can collaborate with fashion brands to offer a wide range of virtual clothing options, including everyday wear, formal attire, and even couture designs. Virtual wardrobes can be regularly updated with new collections, ensuring that users have access to the latest fashion trends.

2.4.2.3 Procedural Generation

Procedural generation is a technique that uses algorithms to generate unique and diverse avatars. By defining a set of rules and parameters, designers can create a system that automatically generates avatars with different body types, facial features, and clothing styles. This technique allows for a high degree of personalization and ensures that each avatar is unique.

2.4.3 Tools for Avatar Personalization

To facilitate avatar personalization, virtual fashion designers can utilize various tools and technologies. Here are some commonly used tools:

2.4.3.1 Avatar Creation Software

Avatar creation software provides designers with a user-friendly interface to design and customize avatars. These tools often include a wide range of options for modifying facial features, body shape, and clothing. They also allow for the import of custom textures and designs, enabling designers to create unique and personalized virtual clothing.

2.4.3.2 Body Scanning Technology

Body scanning technology allows users to create avatars that closely resemble their real-world bodies. This technology uses 3D scanning techniques to capture accurate body measurements, which can then be used to create a virtual representation. By incorporating body scanning technology, designers can offer a more realistic and personalized avatar creation experience.

2.4.3.3 Machine Learning Algorithms

Machine learning algorithms can be used to analyze user preferences and generate personalized recommendations for avatar customization. By collecting data on user interactions and preferences, designers can create algorithms that suggest clothing styles, colors, and accessories that align with each user's unique taste. This technology enhances the personalization experience and helps users discover new fashion options.

2.4.4 Future Trends in Avatar Personalization

As virtual fashion continues to evolve, we can expect to see even more advanced techniques and tools for avatar personalization. Here are some future trends to watch out for:

2.4.4.1 Virtual Reality Integration

Virtual reality (VR) technology is becoming increasingly popular, and its integration with avatar personalization is an exciting prospect. VR allows users to fully immerse themselves in virtual environments, and by incorporating avatar personalization into VR experiences, users can have a more realistic and engaging fashion experience.

2.4.4.2 Artificial Intelligence Assistance

Artificial intelligence (AI) can play a significant role in avatar personalization. AI algorithms can analyze user data and preferences to generate personalized recommendations for clothing and accessories. Additionally, AI can assist in the creation of virtual clothing by automatically adjusting designs to fit different body types and sizes.

2.4.4.3 Social Media Integration

Social media platforms are already influential in the fashion industry, and their integration with avatar personalization can further enhance the virtual fashion experience. By allowing users to share their virtual fashion creations on social media, designers can create a community of fashion enthusiasts who can inspire and support each other's personal style.

In conclusion, avatar personalization is a crucial aspect of virtual fashion design. By offering a wide range of customization options and utilizing advanced tools and technologies, designers can create a truly immersive and personalized fashion experience for users. As virtual fashion continues to evolve, we can expect to see even more innovative techniques and trends in avatar personalization, further blurring the lines between the virtual and real-world fashion.

3 Virtual Couture Design

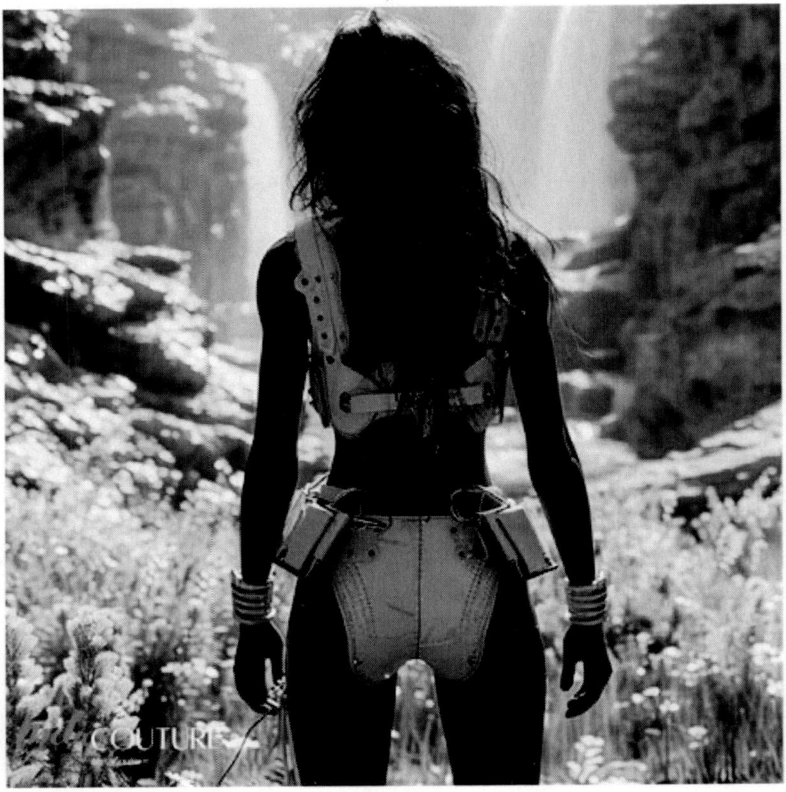

3.1 The Art of Couture

Couture fashion has always been synonymous with luxury, craftsmanship, and exclusivity. It represents the pinnacle of fashion design, where garments are meticulously handcrafted with the utmost attention to detail. In the world of virtual fashion, the art of couture takes on a whole new dimension. Designing couture fashion for avatars in the future requires a unique set of skills and a deep understanding of the virtual landscape.

3.1.1 The Essence of Couture

At its core, couture is about creating one-of-a-kind pieces that are tailored to perfection. It is an art form that celebrates individuality and self-expression. In the virtual realm, the essence of couture remains the same, but the canvas on which it is created is different. Avatars provide designers with endless possibilities to experiment and push the boundaries of fashion.

3.1.2 Translating Couture to Avatars

Adapting couture for avatars requires a careful balance between traditional craftsmanship and digital innovation. Designers must consider the unique characteristics of avatars, such as their virtual body measurements and the limitations of virtual fabric simulation. The goal is to create garments that not only look stunning but also move and drape realistically on the avatar's digital form.

To achieve this, designers can leverage advanced 3D modeling and simulation technologies. These tools allow them to visualize how the garment will look and behave in the virtual environment. By simulating the fabric's movement and interaction with the avatar's body, designers can ensure that the couture piece retains its elegance and grace.

3.1.3 Pushing the Boundaries of Virtual Fabric

In traditional couture, fabric selection plays a crucial role in the overall design. The same holds true for virtual couture. Designers must carefully choose virtual fabrics that not only look visually appealing but also behave realistically in the virtual world. Virtual fabrics can range from silk and satin to more unconventional materials like holographic or luminescent textiles.

Virtual fabric selection also opens up new possibilities for experimentation. Designers can create fabrics that change color or pattern in response to the avatar's movements or the virtual environment. They can also explore the use of textures and embellishments that would be impossible or impractical in the physical world.

3.1.4 Mastering Virtual Couture Techniques

Virtual couture techniques go beyond traditional sewing and draping. Designers must familiarize themselves with digital tools and software specifically designed for virtual fashion design. These tools allow them to manipulate virtual fabrics, create intricate patterns, and apply realistic textures.

One of the key techniques in virtual couture is the ability to create garments that adapt to the avatar's body. This involves using algorithms and simulations to ensure that the garment fits perfectly and moves naturally with the avatar's movements. Designers can also experiment with different silhouettes and proportions, pushing the boundaries of what is possible in the physical world.

3.1.5 Enhancing Couture with Virtual Accessories

Accessories are an integral part of couture fashion, and the same holds true for virtual couture. Designers can create virtual accessories that complement and enhance the overall look of the garment. These accessories can range from jewelry and handbags to virtual props and even virtual makeup.

Virtual accessories offer designers the opportunity to experiment with unconventional materials and designs. They can create accessories that defy gravity or change shape in response to the avatar's movements. The possibilities are endless, limited only by the designer's imagination.

3.1.6 Showcasing Virtual Couture

Fashion shows have always been a platform for designers to showcase their couture creations. In the virtual world, fashion shows take on a whole new dimension. Designers can create immersive virtual environments where avatars walk the runway, showcasing their couture pieces to a global audience.

Virtual fashion shows offer designers the opportunity to experiment with lighting, sound, and special effects, creating a truly unique and unforgettable experience. They can also collaborate with virtual set designers, choreographers, and music producers to create a cohesive and captivating show.

In conclusion, designing couture fashion for avatars in the future requires a deep understanding of the art of couture and the unique challenges and opportunities presented by the virtual world. It is a fusion of traditional craftsmanship and digital innovation, where designers push the boundaries of fashion and self-expression. By embracing the art of couture in the virtual realm, designers can create truly extraordinary and transformative fashion experiences.

3.2 Adapting Couture for Avatars

As the world of fashion continues to evolve, the rise of virtual fashion and the emergence of avatars have opened up new possibilities for designers. Couture, known for its exquisite craftsmanship and attention to detail, is no exception. Adapting couture for avatars requires a unique understanding of both the traditional art of couture and the digital realm. In this section, we will explore the process of adapting couture for avatars and the skills needed to excel in this futuristic field.

Understanding the Essence of Couture

Before delving into the adaptation of couture for avatars, it is crucial to grasp the essence of couture itself. Couture is the epitome of luxury and craftsmanship, characterized by hand-sewn garments, intricate embellishments, and custom fittings. It is a form of art that celebrates individuality and pushes the boundaries of fashion. To adapt couture for avatars, designers must preserve the essence of couture while embracing the unique challenges and opportunities presented by the digital medium.

Bridging the Gap: Traditional Couture and Virtual Fashion

Adapting couture for avatars requires a delicate balance between traditional couture techniques and the capabilities of virtual fashion. Designers must understand the principles of draping, pattern-making, and garment construction that have been honed over centuries in the world of couture. At the same time, they must explore the possibilities offered by virtual fashion technologies, such as 3D modeling and simulation, to bring their designs to life in the digital realm.

Customization and Personalization

One of the advantages of designing couture for avatars is the ability to offer unparalleled customization and personalization. Avatars can be tailored to individual body measurements, allowing for a perfect fit and eliminating the need for alterations. Designers can create virtual garments that adapt to the avatar's movements and preferences, offering a truly unique and immersive fashion experience. The challenge lies in striking a balance between personalization and maintaining the integrity of the designer's vision.

Virtual Fabric Selection

In the world of couture, fabric selection plays a crucial role in bringing a design to life. Similarly, in the realm of avatars, virtual fabric selection is a vital aspect of adapting couture. Designers must consider the visual and tactile qualities of virtual fabrics, ensuring that they accurately mimic the look and feel of real fabrics. The choice of virtual fabrics can greatly impact the overall aesthetic and perception of the garment, making it essential for designers to have a deep understanding of both traditional and virtual textiles.

Techniques for Virtual Couture

Adapting couture techniques for avatars requires a reimagining of traditional craftsmanship in the digital space. Designers must explore innovative ways to create virtual garments that capture the essence of couture. This may involve utilizing digital tools for draping, pattern-making, and embellishment, as well as experimenting with new techniques unique to the virtual realm. The challenge lies in seamlessly blending the artistry of couture with the technical capabilities of virtual fashion.

Virtual Couture Accessories

Accessories are an integral part of couture fashion, adding the finishing touches to a design. In the virtual world, designers have the opportunity to create accessories that defy the limitations of physical materials. Virtual couture accessories can be bold, intricate, and ethereal, enhancing the overall aesthetic of the avatar's ensemble. Designers can experiment with unconventional materials, shapes, and textures, pushing the boundaries of traditional accessory design.

Virtual Couture Fashion Shows

Fashion shows have long been a platform for designers to showcase their couture creations. In the virtual realm, fashion shows take on a whole new dimension. Virtual couture fashion shows offer designers the freedom to create immersive and interactive experiences for their audience. Avatars can walk the virtual runway, showcasing the intricate details and craftsmanship of the couture designs. Designers can experiment with lighting, sound, and special effects to create a truly unforgettable spectacle.

Embracing the Future of Couture

Adapting couture for avatars requires a willingness to embrace the future of fashion. Designers must be open to exploring new technologies, learning digital tools, and collaborating with experts in the field of virtual fashion. The future of couture lies in the seamless integration of traditional craftsmanship and digital innovation. By embracing this future, designers can push the boundaries of their creativity and create couture designs that transcend the physical realm.

In conclusion, adapting couture for avatars is a fascinating and challenging endeavor. It requires a deep understanding of the art of couture, as well as a willingness to explore the possibilities offered by virtual fashion technologies. Designers must strike a balance between preserving the essence of couture and embracing the unique opportunities presented by the digital medium. By mastering the skills needed to adapt couture for avatars and embracing the future of fashion, designers can pave the way for a new era of virtual couture.

3.3 Virtual Fabric Selection

When it comes to designing couture fashion for avatars in the virtual world, one of the most important aspects to consider is the selection of virtual fabrics. Just like in the physical world, the choice of fabric plays a crucial role in the overall look and feel of the garment. However, in the virtual realm, designers have the freedom to explore a wide range of materials that may not be possible or practical in the real world.

3.3.1 Understanding Virtual Fabrics

Virtual fabrics are digital representations of different materials that can be applied to the surface of virtual garments. These fabrics are created using advanced computer graphics techniques and can mimic the appearance, texture, and behavior of real fabrics. From silk and satin to leather and denim, virtual fabrics can replicate a vast array of materials, allowing designers to experiment with different looks and styles.

3.3.2 Factors to Consider in Virtual Fabric Selection

When selecting virtual fabrics for couture designs, there are several factors that designers need to take into consideration:

3.3.2.1 Aesthetic Appeal

The aesthetic appeal of a fabric is of utmost importance in fashion design. In the virtual world, designers have the advantage of being able to create fabrics that are visually stunning and unique.

They can experiment with vibrant colors, intricate patterns, and unconventional textures to create garments that stand out and make a statement.

3.3.2.2 Realism

While virtual fabrics offer endless possibilities, it is important to strike a balance between creativity and realism. The fabric should look and behave in a way that is believable to the viewer. For example, if a designer wants to create a flowing gown, the virtual fabric should have the appearance and movement of a lightweight material such as chiffon or silk.

3.3.2.3 Compatibility with Avatar Body

Another crucial factor to consider is how the virtual fabric interacts with the avatar's body. The fabric should drape and conform to the avatar's shape in a natural and realistic manner. Designers need to ensure that the fabric behaves correctly when the avatar moves, bends, or sits down. This requires careful consideration of the fabric's physical properties and how it interacts with the virtual environment.

3.3.2.4 Performance and Optimization

Virtual fashion design involves creating garments that can be rendered in real-time on various devices and platforms. Therefore, designers need to consider the performance and optimization of the virtual fabrics they choose. High-resolution textures and complex shaders may look visually appealing, but they can also impact the performance of the virtual fashion experience. Finding a balance between visual quality and performance is essential.

3.3.3 Types of Virtual Fabrics

In the virtual fashion world, there is a wide range of virtual fabrics to choose from. Here are some common types of virtual fabrics that designers can explore:

3.3.3.1 Synthetic Fabrics

Synthetic fabrics such as polyester, nylon, and spandex are popular choices in virtual fashion design. These fabrics offer versatility and can be easily manipulated to create different shapes and forms. They are often used for creating futuristic and avant-garde designs that push the boundaries of traditional fashion.

3.3.3.2 Natural Fabrics

Natural fabrics like cotton, silk, and wool can also be replicated in the virtual world. These fabrics have a timeless appeal and are often used for creating classic and elegant designs. The virtual versions of these fabrics can capture the softness, sheen, and texture of the real materials, adding a touch of realism to the virtual garments.

3.3.3.3 Fantasy Fabrics

In the virtual realm, designers have the freedom to create fabrics that defy the laws of physics. Fantasy fabrics such as holographic materials, iridescent fabrics, and glowing textiles can add a touch of magic and whimsy to virtual couture designs. These fabrics allow designers to unleash their creativity and create garments that are truly unique and otherworldly.

3.3.4 Virtual Fabric Creation Process

Creating virtual fabrics involves a combination of artistic creativity and technical expertise. Here is a general overview of the virtual fabric creation process:

1. Research and Inspiration: Designers start by researching different fabrics and gathering inspiration from various sources such as fashion magazines, fabric swatches, and online resources.
2. Texture Mapping: The next step is to create a high-resolution texture map that captures the visual details of the fabric. This includes the color, pattern, and texture of the material.
3. Shading and Lighting: Designers then apply shaders and lighting techniques to the virtual fabric to enhance its appearance and simulate how it reacts to different lighting conditions.
4. Physics Simulation: To achieve realistic movement and behavior, designers can use physics simulation techniques to simulate the physical properties of the fabric, such as elasticity, stiffness, and gravity.
5. Testing and Refinement: Once the virtual fabric is created, designers test it on different avatars and in various virtual

environments to ensure that it looks and behaves as intended. Any necessary adjustments or refinements are made during this stage.

3.3.5 Virtual Fabric Libraries

To streamline the virtual fashion design process, designers can make use of virtual fabric libraries. These libraries contain a collection of pre-designed virtual fabrics that can be easily applied to garments. Designers can browse through the library, select the desired fabric, and apply it to their designs, saving time and effort in the creation process.

Virtual fabric libraries often include a wide range of materials, patterns, and textures, allowing designers to experiment with different looks and styles. They can also be customized and modified to suit specific design requirements, giving designers even more flexibility and creative control.

In conclusion, virtual fabric selection is a crucial aspect of designing couture fashion for avatars in the virtual world. Designers have the freedom to explore a wide range of materials, textures, and patterns, creating garments that are visually stunning and unique. By considering factors such as aesthetic appeal, realism, compatibility with avatars, and performance optimization, designers can create virtual fabrics that enhance the overall virtual fashion experience. With the help of virtual fabric libraries and the use of advanced computer graphics techniques, designers can bring their couture visions to life in the virtual realm.

3.4 Virtual Couture Techniques

In the world of virtual fashion, couture design takes on a whole new level of creativity and innovation. Designers have the opportunity to push the boundaries of traditional fashion and explore new techniques that are only possible in the virtual realm. Virtual couture techniques allow designers to create unique and intricate garments that are tailored specifically for avatars. In this section, we will explore some of the techniques used in virtual couture design and how designers can prepare for the future of this exciting field.

3.4.1 Virtual Draping and Pattern Making

One of the fundamental techniques in couture design is draping, which involves manipulating fabric directly on a dress form to create the desired shape and silhouette. In the virtual world, designers can use digital tools to simulate the draping process. Virtual draping allows designers to experiment with different fabric weights, textures, and drape effects without the need for physical materials. This technique enables designers to visualize their designs in real-time and make adjustments easily.

Pattern making is another essential aspect of couture design. In the virtual realm, designers can create digital patterns that are tailored specifically for avatars. These patterns can be adjusted and modified to fit different body types and sizes. Virtual pattern making tools provide designers with precise measurements and allow for quick iterations and adjustments. This digital approach to pattern making saves time and resources compared to traditional methods.

3.4.2 Virtual Embroidery and Embellishments

Embroidery and embellishments are often used to add intricate details and textures to couture garments. In the virtual world, designers can explore a wide range of digital embroidery techniques to create stunning and unique designs. Virtual embroidery tools allow designers to experiment with different stitch patterns, thread colors, and embellishments without the limitations of physical materials. This opens up endless possibilities for creating intricate and elaborate designs that would be challenging to achieve in the physical world.

3.4.3 Virtual Texturing and Material Simulation

Texturing and material simulation play a crucial role in bringing virtual couture designs to life. Designers can use digital tools to apply realistic textures and materials to their virtual garments. These tools allow designers to experiment with different fabric types, finishes, and colors, giving them the ability to create visually stunning and realistic virtual garments. Virtual material simulation also enables designers to simulate the behavior of different fabrics, such as how they drape, flow, or reflect light. This level of realism enhances the overall virtual couture experience.

3.4.4 Virtual Fitting and Tailoring

One of the challenges in traditional fashion design is achieving the perfect fit for each individual body shape. In the virtual world, designers can overcome this challenge by using virtual fitting and tailoring techniques. Virtual fitting tools allow designers to adjust the fit of garments on avatars in real-time. Designers can modify the length, width, and proportions of the garments to ensure a perfect fit for each avatar. This level of customization and personalization is one of the key advantages of virtual couture design.

3.4.5 Virtual Collaboration and Co-Creation

Virtual couture design also opens up new opportunities for collaboration and co-creation. Designers can work together in virtual environments, sharing ideas, and collaborating on designs in real-time. Virtual collaboration tools allow designers to communicate and work together regardless of their physical location. This level of collaboration fosters creativity and innovation, as designers can draw inspiration from each other and combine their skills and expertise to create unique and groundbreaking virtual couture designs.

3.4.6 Virtual Couture Design Workflow

To effectively utilize virtual couture techniques, designers need to establish a streamlined workflow that integrates digital tools and processes. This workflow should include steps such as avatar customization, virtual draping and pattern making, virtual embroidery and embellishments, virtual texturing and material simulation, virtual fitting and tailoring, and virtual collaboration. By following a structured workflow, designers can maximize their efficiency and creativity in virtual couture design.

3.4.7 Preparing for the Future of Virtual Couture

As virtual fashion continues to evolve, it is essential for designers to stay updated with the latest technologies and trends. Designers should invest in learning and mastering virtual design tools and techniques. They should also keep an eye on emerging technologies such as virtual reality and augmented reality, as these technologies have the potential to revolutionize the virtual couture industry. Additionally, designers should embrace a mindset of continuous learning and adaptability to stay ahead in this rapidly changing field.

In conclusion, virtual couture techniques offer designers a world of possibilities in creating unique and innovative fashion for avatars. From virtual draping and pattern making to virtual embroidery and embellishments, these techniques allow designers to push the boundaries of traditional fashion and explore new creative avenues. By embracing virtual couture and preparing for the future of this exciting field, designers can stay at the forefront of the virtual fashion industry and create groundbreaking designs that captivate audiences worldwide.

3.5 Virtual Couture Accessories

In the world of virtual fashion, accessories play a crucial role in completing the overall look and enhancing the style of avatars. Just like in the physical world, virtual couture accessories add that extra touch of glamour, sophistication, and personalization to virtual outfits. From statement jewelry to handbags, hats, and shoes, virtual couture accessories offer endless possibilities for designers to showcase their creativity and elevate the virtual fashion experience.

3.5.1 The Importance of Virtual Couture Accessories

Virtual couture accessories are not just decorative elements; they serve a purpose in enhancing the avatar's appearance and expressing their personality. These accessories can be used to create a specific theme or style, adding depth and character to the virtual fashion ensemble. Whether it's a bold statement necklace, a delicate pair of earrings, or a stylish handbag, accessories have the power to transform an avatar's look from ordinary to extraordinary.

3.5.2 Designing Virtual Couture Accessories

Designing virtual couture accessories requires a combination of creativity, technical skills, and an understanding of the virtual fashion landscape. Just like in traditional fashion design, designers need to consider factors such as color, texture, shape, and proportion when creating accessories for avatars. However, there are some unique considerations when designing for the virtual world.

One of the advantages of virtual couture accessories is the ability to experiment with unconventional materials and shapes that may not be feasible in the physical world. Designers can push the boundaries of creativity by using holographic materials, futuristic shapes, and intricate details that would be challenging to achieve in traditional fashion. Virtual couture accessories can be designed to defy gravity, change colors, or even emit light, creating a truly immersive and magical experience for the avatar and the viewer.

3.5.3 Customization and Personalization

Virtual couture accessories offer a high level of customization and personalization, allowing avatars to express their individuality and style. Designers can create accessories that can be easily modified, resized, and adapted to suit different avatars' preferences. This level of customization ensures that each avatar can have a unique and personalized fashion experience.

Furthermore, virtual couture accessories can be designed to interact with the avatar's movements and environment. For example, a virtual handbag can have animated elements that sway with the avatar's movements or change color based on the virtual environment's lighting conditions. These interactive features add an extra layer of engagement and immersion to the virtual fashion experience.

3.5.4 Collaboration with Virtual Fashion Designers

Designing virtual couture accessories often involves collaboration with virtual fashion designers. By working together, designers can create cohesive and harmonious virtual fashion ensembles that seamlessly integrate accessories with garments. Collaboration allows for a holistic approach to virtual fashion design, ensuring that every element of the avatar's outfit complements each other and creates a visually stunning and cohesive look.

Virtual fashion designers can provide valuable insights into the overall aesthetic and style of the avatar, helping accessory designers align their creations with the desired look. This collaboration also opens up opportunities for cross-promotion and cross-selling, as virtual fashion designers can showcase the accessories alongside their garments, creating a complete virtual fashion collection.

3.5.5 Virtual Couture Accessories in Virtual Fashion Shows

Virtual fashion shows provide a platform for designers to showcase their virtual couture accessories to a global audience. These shows are not limited by physical constraints and can be held in virtual environments that reflect the designer's vision and theme. Virtual fashion shows allow designers to experiment with innovative presentation formats, such as holographic runways, interactive stages, and immersive virtual environments.

During virtual fashion shows, accessories can take center stage, with models showcasing the intricate details and craftsmanship of each piece. Designers can leverage technology to create dynamic presentations, where accessories come to life through animations, special effects, and virtual interactions. Virtual fashion shows offer a unique opportunity for designers to captivate the audience and leave a lasting impression with their virtual couture accessories.

3.5.6 Future Trends in Virtual Couture Accessories

As virtual fashion continues to evolve, so will the trends in virtual couture accessories. Here are some potential future trends to watch out for:

1. **Sustainable Virtual Accessories**: With the growing focus on sustainability, designers may explore eco-friendly materials and production methods for virtual couture accessories. This could include using recycled virtual fabrics, incorporating virtual upcycling techniques, or even designing accessories that promote virtual environmental awareness.
2. **Virtual Reality Integration**: Virtual couture accessories could be designed to integrate seamlessly with virtual reality experiences. For example, accessories could enhance the virtual reality immersion by providing haptic feedback or interacting with the virtual environment in unique ways.
3. **Virtual Couture Tech Accessories**: As technology advances, virtual couture accessories could incorporate wearable technology elements. This could include accessories with built-in virtual reality displays, interactive touch surfaces, or even accessories that can communicate with other virtual devices.
4. **Collaborative Virtual Accessories**: Virtual couture accessories could be designed to encourage collaboration and social interaction within virtual environments. For example, accessories that allow avatars to share virtual content, exchange virtual gifts, or even create virtual fashion trends together.

The future of virtual couture accessories is full of exciting possibilities. As designers continue to push the boundaries of creativity and technology, we can expect to see even more innovative and captivating accessories that will redefine the virtual fashion landscape. By embracing these trends and preparing for the future, designers can stay at the forefront of the virtual fashion industry and create unforgettable virtual fashion experiences for avatars and fashion enthusiasts alike.

3.6 Virtual Couture Fashion Shows

Fashion shows have always been a significant part of the fashion industry, showcasing the latest trends and designs to the world. In the world of virtual fashion, couture fashion shows take on a whole new dimension. These virtual events provide a platform for designers to showcase their creations on avatars, allowing them to push the boundaries of creativity and imagination.

The Evolution of Virtual Couture Fashion Shows

Virtual couture fashion shows have come a long way since their inception. Initially, they were simple presentations of digital garments on virtual models. However, with advancements in technology, these shows have become immersive experiences that rival traditional fashion shows.

One of the key advantages of virtual couture fashion shows is the ability to create a unique and captivating environment. Designers can create virtual worlds that complement their collections, transporting the audience to a different realm. From futuristic cityscapes to enchanted forests, the possibilities are endless.

The Experience of Virtual Couture Fashion Shows

Attending a virtual couture fashion show is a truly immersive experience. Participants can access the show from the comfort of their own homes, eliminating the need for travel and physical attendance. They can explore the virtual venue, interact with other attendees, and even try on virtual garments themselves.

During the show, avatars walk down the virtual runway, showcasing the designer's creations. The avatars can be customized to reflect the desired aesthetic, allowing designers to experiment with different body types, skin tones, and even non-human forms. This level of customization adds a new layer of creativity and inclusivity to the fashion industry.

Virtual couture fashion shows also offer unique opportunities for audience engagement. Viewers can interact with the avatars, zoom in on the garments for a closer look, and even purchase virtual versions of the designs. This level of interactivity enhances the overall experience and creates a sense of connection between the designer and the audience.

Designing for Virtual Couture Fashion Shows

Designing for virtual couture fashion shows requires a different approach compared to traditional fashion shows. Designers must consider the limitations and possibilities of the virtual environment, ensuring that their creations translate well onto avatars.

One of the key considerations is the movement of the garments. Virtual garments need to be designed to move realistically on avatars, taking into account factors such as gravity and fabric physics. Designers can utilize simulation software to test the movement of their designs before the show, ensuring that they flow and drape naturally.

Another important aspect is the use of virtual fabrics. Designers have the freedom to experiment with materials that may not be feasible in the physical world. From holographic textiles to ethereal fabrics that defy gravity, virtual couture allows for the exploration of unconventional materials and textures.

Additionally, designers must pay attention to the details of their virtual garments. Since the audience can zoom in and examine the designs up close, every stitch, embellishment, and texture must be meticulously crafted. The level of detail in virtual couture is often unparalleled, allowing designers to create intricate and awe-inspiring pieces.

Collaboration and Innovation in Virtual Couture Fashion Shows

Virtual couture fashion shows also foster collaboration and innovation within the fashion industry. Designers can collaborate with virtual artists, animators, and programmers to bring their visions to life. This interdisciplinary approach allows for the integration of technology and artistry, resulting in groundbreaking and visually stunning shows.

Furthermore, virtual couture fashion shows provide a platform for emerging designers to showcase their talent. The accessibility and global reach of virtual shows enable designers from all corners of the world to participate and gain exposure. This democratization of the fashion industry opens doors for new voices and perspectives to be heard.

Preparing for the Future of Virtual Couture Fashion Shows

As virtual fashion continues to evolve, it is essential for designers to stay ahead of the curve and prepare for the future of virtual couture fashion shows. This involves embracing new technologies, honing digital design skills, and understanding the potential of virtual reality and augmented reality.

Designers should also consider the sustainability aspect of virtual couture. Virtual fashion shows have the potential to reduce the environmental impact associated with traditional fashion shows, such as travel and waste. By embracing virtual couture, designers can contribute to a more sustainable and eco-friendly fashion industry.

In conclusion, virtual couture fashion shows offer a new and exciting platform for designers to showcase their creativity and push the boundaries of fashion. These immersive experiences provide a unique opportunity for audience engagement and collaboration. By embracing virtual couture, designers can prepare themselves for the future of the fashion industry and contribute to its continued evolution.

4 Virtual Fashion Technology

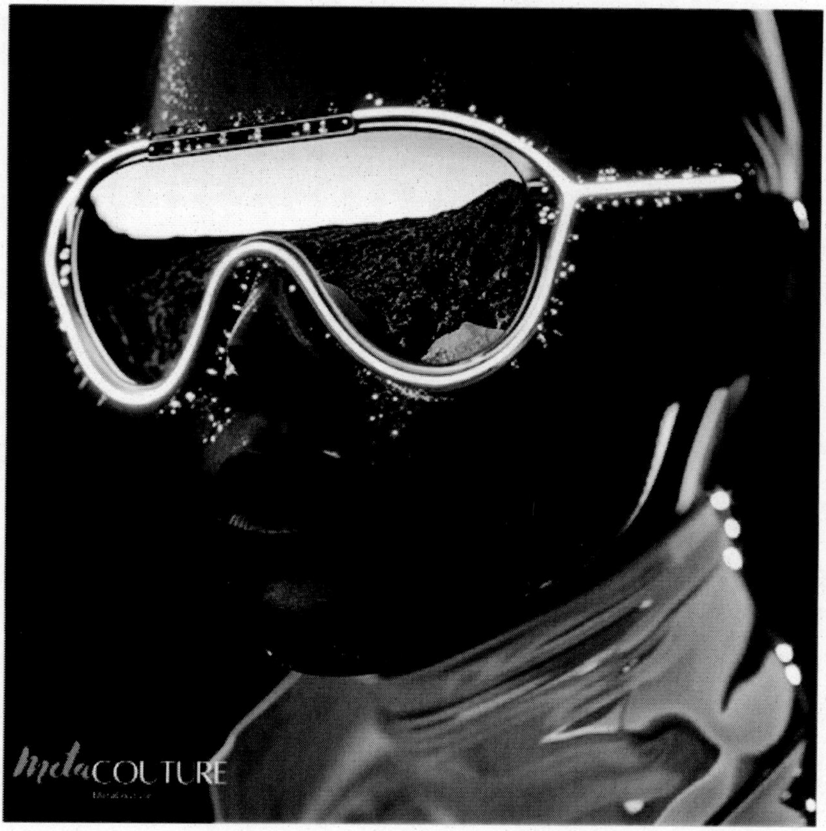

4.1 Virtual Reality and Fashion

Virtual reality (VR) has revolutionized various industries, and the fashion world is no exception. With the advancement of technology, designers are now able to create immersive and interactive experiences for fashion enthusiasts through virtual reality. This chapter explores the intersection of virtual reality and fashion, highlighting the potential it holds for the future of the industry.

4.1.1 The Power of Virtual Reality in Fashion

Virtual reality offers a unique platform for fashion designers to showcase their creations in a way that was previously unimaginable. By creating virtual environments, designers can transport users into a world where they can interact with and experience fashion in a whole new way. Virtual reality allows for a level of engagement and personalization that traditional fashion shows or photographs cannot provide.

One of the key advantages of virtual reality in fashion is the ability to create virtual fashion shows. Designers can create immersive catwalk experiences where users can virtually attend and interact with the show. This opens up new possibilities for showcasing collections to a global audience without the limitations of physical space or time. Virtual fashion shows also allow designers to experiment with unconventional settings and themes, creating a truly unique and memorable experience for viewers.

4.1.2 Virtual Reality and Fashion Design

Virtual reality technology has also transformed the design process itself. Designers can now create virtual prototypes of their garments, allowing them to visualize and refine their designs before producing physical samples. This not only saves time and resources but also enables designers to experiment with different materials, colors, and patterns without the need for physical materials.

Furthermore, virtual reality enables designers to collaborate more effectively. With the ability to share virtual environments, multiple designers can work together in real-time, regardless of their physical location. This opens up opportunities for cross-cultural collaborations and the exchange of ideas, ultimately leading to more innovative and diverse fashion designs.

4.1.3 Virtual Reality and Consumer Experience

Virtual reality has the potential to revolutionize the way consumers experience fashion. With virtual reality headsets becoming more accessible, consumers can now virtually try on clothes and accessories from the comfort of their own homes. This not only enhances the convenience of online shopping but also reduces the need for physical try-ons, minimizing the environmental impact of the fashion industry.

Virtual reality also allows consumers to personalize their virtual avatars, creating a more immersive and engaging shopping experience. By inputting their body measurements and preferences, consumers can see how different garments would look on their virtual avatars, helping them make more informed purchasing decisions.

4.1.4 Challenges and Considerations

While virtual reality holds immense potential for the future of fashion, there are also challenges and considerations that need to be addressed. One of the main challenges is the cost and accessibility of virtual reality technology. Although virtual reality headsets are becoming more affordable, they are still not widely accessible to the general public. Additionally, creating high-quality virtual environments and avatars requires specialized skills and resources, which may pose a barrier for smaller fashion brands or independent designers.

Another consideration is the ethical implications of virtual fashion. As virtual fashion becomes more prevalent, there is a need to ensure that virtual garments are not used to promote unrealistic body standards or perpetuate harmful beauty ideals. Designers and industry stakeholders must prioritize inclusivity and diversity in virtual fashion, ensuring that all body types and identities are represented and celebrated.

4.1.5 The Future of Virtual Reality and Fashion

The future of virtual reality and fashion is promising. As technology continues to advance, virtual reality experiences will become more immersive and realistic. Virtual fashion shows may become a mainstream alternative to physical shows, allowing designers to reach a global audience without the need for travel or large-scale events. Virtual reality shopping experiences will become more seamless and personalized, enhancing the overall consumer experience.

In order to prepare for the future of virtual fashion, designers need to embrace and adapt to new technologies. This includes acquiring the necessary skills and knowledge in virtual reality design and development. Fashion schools and educational institutions should incorporate virtual reality into their curriculum, ensuring that future designers are equipped with the tools and expertise to thrive in the virtual fashion industry.

Collaboration will also play a crucial role in the future of virtual fashion. Designers, technologists, and industry professionals need to work together to push the boundaries of virtual reality and fashion, exploring new possibilities and creating innovative experiences. By embracing virtual reality as a tool for creativity and expression, the fashion industry can continue to evolve and adapt to the changing landscape of technology.

In conclusion, virtual reality has the potential to revolutionize the fashion industry. From virtual fashion shows to immersive shopping experiences, virtual reality offers new avenues for creativity, engagement, and personalization. However, it is important to address the challenges and considerations associated with virtual fashion, ensuring inclusivity, accessibility, and ethical practices. By embracing virtual reality and preparing for the future, fashion designers can stay at the forefront of innovation and shape the future of the industry.

4.2 Augmented Reality and Fashion

Augmented reality (AR) has become an increasingly popular technology in recent years, revolutionizing various industries, including fashion. AR combines the virtual world with the real world, enhancing our perception and interaction with our surroundings. In the context of fashion, AR opens up exciting possibilities for designers to create immersive and interactive experiences for their customers.

4.2.1 Enhancing the Shopping Experience

One of the key applications of AR in fashion is enhancing the shopping experience for customers. With AR, fashion brands can create virtual fitting rooms where customers can try on clothes virtually without physically being present in a store. This allows customers to see how different outfits would look on them before making a purchase, saving time and reducing the need for returns.

AR also enables customers to visualize how accessories, such as jewelry or handbags, would complement their outfits. By simply pointing their smartphone or tablet at themselves, customers can see a virtual overlay of the accessory on their body, helping them make more informed purchasing decisions.

4.2.2 Virtual Styling and Personalization

AR technology can also be used to provide personalized styling recommendations to customers. By analyzing a customer's body shape, skin tone, and personal preferences, AR can generate virtual outfits that are tailored to their individual style. This not only helps customers discover new fashion trends but also allows them to experiment with different looks without the need to physically try on multiple garments.

Furthermore, AR can enable customers to virtually try on different hairstyles, makeup looks, and even experiment with different colors and patterns for their clothing. This level of personalization enhances the overall shopping experience and empowers customers to express their unique style.

4.2.3 Virtual Fashion Shows and Runways

AR has the potential to transform the way fashion shows and runways are conducted. With AR, designers can create virtual fashion shows that can be accessed by anyone with a compatible device. This opens up the possibility of reaching a global audience without the limitations of physical venues.

Virtual fashion shows can be designed to be interactive, allowing viewers to explore the garments in detail, change the color or fabric, and even purchase items directly from the show. This not only increases engagement but also provides designers with valuable data on customer preferences and trends.

4.2.4 Virtual Try-On and Customization

AR technology enables customers to virtually try on clothes and customize them according to their preferences. By using their smartphone or tablet, customers can see how a garment would look on them in real-time, adjusting the fit, color, and style to suit their individual taste.

Virtual try-on and customization not only enhances the shopping experience but also reduces the environmental impact of fashion by minimizing the need for physical production and transportation of garments. This technology allows customers to make more sustainable choices by only purchasing items they truly love and will wear.

4.2.5 Collaborative Design and Feedback

AR can facilitate collaboration between designers, manufacturers, and customers. By using AR tools, designers can create virtual prototypes of their designs, allowing stakeholders to provide feedback and make adjustments before the physical production process begins. This streamlines the design process, reduces costs, and ensures that the final product meets customer expectations.

Furthermore, AR can enable customers to actively participate in the design process by allowing them to customize and personalize garments according to their preferences. This level of collaboration not only strengthens the relationship between designers and customers but also creates a sense of ownership and uniqueness for the customers.

4.2.6 The Future of Augmented Reality and Fashion

As technology continues to advance, the future of AR in fashion looks promising. We can expect to see more seamless integration of AR into our everyday lives, with wearable AR devices becoming more common. This will further enhance the shopping experience, allowing customers to access AR features without the need for a separate device.

Additionally, advancements in AR technology will enable more realistic and immersive virtual experiences, blurring the line between the physical and virtual worlds. This will open up new possibilities for designers to push the boundaries of creativity and create truly unique and captivating fashion experiences.

In conclusion, augmented reality has the potential to revolutionize the fashion industry by enhancing the shopping experience, enabling virtual styling and personalization, transforming fashion shows, facilitating virtual try-on and customization, promoting collaboration, and shaping the future of fashion. As designers, it is essential to embrace and adapt to these technological advancements to stay relevant and thrive in the ever-evolving world of virtual fashion.

4.3 3D Modeling and Simulation

In the world of virtual fashion, 3D modeling and simulation play a crucial role in bringing couture designs to life for avatars. This technology allows fashion designers to create intricate and detailed garments that can be visualized and tested in a virtual environment before they are produced in the physical world. In this section, we will explore the importance of 3D modeling and simulation in virtual fashion design and how it can revolutionize the way couture is created for avatars.

4.3.1 The Power of 3D Modeling

3D modeling is the process of creating a three-dimensional representation of an object using specialized software. In the context of virtual fashion, 3D modeling allows designers to digitally construct garments with precision and accuracy. By using virtual mannequins or avatars as a base, designers can drape, shape, and manipulate virtual fabrics to create unique and innovative couture designs.

One of the key advantages of 3D modeling is the ability to visualize the garment from all angles. Designers can rotate, zoom in, and zoom out to examine every detail of the garment, ensuring that it meets their vision and specifications. This level of control and flexibility is not easily achievable in traditional fashion design, where designers often have to rely on physical prototypes and multiple fittings to achieve the desired result.

4.3.2 Simulation for Realistic Virtual Couture

Simulation is an integral part of the 3D modeling process in virtual fashion design. It allows designers to test the functionality and movement of the garments on avatars, simulating real-life scenarios. By applying physics-based algorithms, designers can simulate the behavior of fabrics, such as draping, folding, and stretching, to ensure that the virtual couture behaves realistically.

Through simulation, designers can also experiment with different fabric properties, such as stiffness, elasticity, and weight, to achieve the desired aesthetic and functionality of the garment. This enables them to explore new design possibilities and push the boundaries of traditional couture.

4.3.3 Advantages of 3D Modeling and Simulation

The use of 3D modeling and simulation in virtual fashion design offers several advantages over traditional methods:

4.3.3.1 Time and Cost Efficiency

By creating virtual prototypes and conducting simulations, designers can significantly reduce the time and cost involved in the design and development process. They can quickly iterate and make adjustments to the design without the need for physical materials or multiple fittings. This not only speeds up the design process but also reduces material waste and production costs.

4.3.3.2 Design Exploration and Innovation

3D modeling and simulation open up a world of possibilities for designers to explore new design concepts and push the boundaries of traditional couture. They can experiment with different fabric combinations, silhouettes, and embellishments without the limitations of physical materials. This encourages creativity and innovation in the virtual fashion industry.

4.3.3.3 Sustainability and Environmental Impact

Virtual fashion design using 3D modeling and simulation has the potential to reduce the environmental impact of the fashion industry. By minimizing the need for physical prototypes and samples, designers can reduce material waste and energy consumption. Additionally, the ability to simulate the behavior of fabrics allows designers to make informed decisions about the sustainability of their designs, such as choosing eco-friendly materials and optimizing garment construction techniques.

4.3.4 Tools and Software for 3D Modeling and Simulation

To harness the power of 3D modeling and simulation in virtual fashion design, designers need access to specialized tools and software. There are several software options available that cater specifically to the needs of fashion designers, offering features such as virtual mannequins, fabric simulation, and realistic rendering.

Some popular 3D modeling and simulation software used in the virtual fashion industry include:

- Marvelous Designer: This software is widely used for creating virtual garments with realistic fabric simulation. It allows designers to drape, sew, and adjust garments on virtual avatars.
- CLO 3D: CLO 3D is another popular software that offers a range of features for virtual fashion design, including pattern-making, fabric simulation, and virtual fitting.

- Browzwear: Browzwear provides a comprehensive suite of tools for 3D modeling, simulation, and visualization of virtual garments. It offers advanced features such as accurate fabric rendering and virtual fitting.

These software tools enable designers to bring their couture designs to life in a virtual environment, allowing for efficient and realistic visualization and simulation.

4.3.5 The Future of 3D Modeling and Simulation in Virtual Fashion

As technology continues to advance, the capabilities of 3D modeling and simulation in virtual fashion design are expected to expand further. With the integration of artificial intelligence and machine learning, designers may be able to automate certain aspects of the design process, such as pattern-making and fabric simulation, making it even more efficient and accessible.

Furthermore, advancements in virtual reality and augmented reality technologies may enable designers to immerse themselves in a virtual environment, where they can interact with their designs in a more intuitive and immersive way. This could revolutionize the way couture is created and experienced, blurring the lines between the physical and virtual worlds.

In conclusion, 3D modeling and simulation are powerful tools that have the potential to transform the way couture fashion is designed for avatars in the future. By enabling designers to visualize, test, and refine their designs in a virtual environment, these technologies offer numerous advantages in terms of time and cost efficiency, design exploration, and sustainability. As the virtual fashion industry continues to evolve, the role of 3D modeling and simulation is expected to become even more prominent, shaping the future of couture fashion for avatars.

4.4 Virtual Fashion Rendering

Virtual fashion rendering is a crucial aspect of designing couture fashion for avatars in the future. It involves creating realistic and visually appealing representations of virtual garments on virtual models. With advancements in technology, virtual fashion rendering has become more sophisticated, allowing designers to showcase their creations in a lifelike manner.

4.4.1 The Importance of Virtual Fashion Rendering

Virtual fashion rendering plays a vital role in the design process as it allows designers to visualize their creations before they are physically produced. It enables them to experiment with different fabrics, colors, and patterns, and make necessary adjustments to achieve the desired aesthetic. By rendering virtual garments on avatars, designers can assess how the clothing will look and fit on different body types, ensuring a more inclusive and diverse representation.

Moreover, virtual fashion rendering allows designers to showcase their collections in a digital format, reaching a wider audience through various online platforms and virtual fashion shows. It provides an opportunity for designers to present their work in a visually captivating and immersive manner, enhancing the overall experience for viewers.

4.4.2 Techniques for Virtual Fashion Rendering

There are several techniques and tools available for virtual fashion rendering, each offering unique features and capabilities. Here are some commonly used techniques:

4.4.2.1 3D Modeling and Simulation

3D modeling is a fundamental technique used in virtual fashion rendering. It involves creating a three-dimensional representation of the garment using specialized software. Designers can manipulate the virtual fabric, drape it on the avatar, and simulate realistic movements to observe how the garment behaves in different scenarios. This technique allows designers to experiment with various design elements, such as silhouette, texture, and embellishments, to achieve the desired look.

4.4.2.2 Texture Mapping

Texture mapping is the process of applying textures, patterns, and colors to the virtual garment. It adds depth and realism to the rendered image, making it visually appealing and lifelike. Designers can choose from a wide range of pre-existing textures or create their own custom textures to achieve the desired effect. Texture mapping is essential for accurately representing different fabric types, such as silk, leather, or lace, and showcasing intricate details like embroidery or prints.

4.4.2.3 Lighting and Shadows

Lighting and shadows play a crucial role in virtual fashion rendering as they contribute to the overall realism of the image. By manipulating the lighting conditions, designers can create different moods and atmospheres, highlighting specific areas of the garment or avatar. Shadows add depth and dimension to the rendered image, making it appear more lifelike. Proper lighting and shadow techniques can enhance the visual impact of the virtual garment, making it more appealing to the audience.

4.4.2.4 Rendering Software

There are various rendering software available that cater specifically to virtual fashion rendering. These software provide designers with a range of tools and features to create realistic and visually stunning renderings. Some popular rendering software include Blender, Marvelous Designer, and KeyShot. These software offer advanced capabilities such as real-time rendering, material editing, and post-processing effects, allowing designers to achieve high-quality renderings.

4.4.3 Challenges in Virtual Fashion Rendering

While virtual fashion rendering offers numerous benefits, there are also challenges that designers may encounter during the process. Some of these challenges include:

4.4.3.1 Realism and Accuracy

Achieving a high level of realism and accuracy in virtual fashion rendering can be challenging. Designers need to ensure that the virtual garment accurately represents the physical garment in terms of color, texture, and fit. It requires attention to detail and a thorough understanding of fabric properties to create a convincing virtual representation.

4.4.3.2 Computational Power

Virtual fashion rendering can be computationally intensive, especially when dealing with complex garments and high-resolution textures. Designers may require powerful hardware and software to handle the rendering process efficiently. The rendering time can vary depending on the complexity of the design and the level of detail required, which may impact the overall workflow and productivity.

4.4.3.3 Collaboration and Communication

Virtual fashion rendering often involves collaboration between designers, pattern makers, and other stakeholders. Effective communication and collaboration are essential to ensure that the virtual garment accurately represents the designer's vision. Clear communication of design details, fabric choices, and desired effects is crucial to achieve the desired outcome.

4.4.4 Future Trends in Virtual Fashion Rendering

As technology continues to advance, virtual fashion rendering is expected to evolve and offer new possibilities for designers. Some future trends in virtual fashion rendering include:

4.4.4.1 Real-time Rendering

Real-time rendering allows designers to see immediate visual feedback as they make changes to the virtual garment. This enables faster iteration and decision-making, enhancing the overall design process. Real-time rendering also facilitates interactive experiences, such as virtual fashion try-ons, where users can see how the garment looks on their personalized avatars in real-time.

4.4.4.2 Photorealistic Rendering

Advancements in rendering software and hardware are enabling designers to achieve photorealistic renderings of virtual garments. With improved lighting and material simulation, virtual garments can closely resemble their physical counterparts. This trend will further blur the line between virtual and physical fashion, providing a more immersive and realistic experience for both designers and consumers.

4.4.4.3 Virtual Reality Integration

Virtual reality (VR) technology is increasingly being integrated into virtual fashion rendering. Designers can create virtual showrooms or virtual fashion experiences where users can interact with the garments in a virtual environment. VR allows for a more immersive and engaging experience, enabling users to explore the virtual garments from different angles and perspectives.

In conclusion, virtual fashion rendering is a crucial aspect of designing couture fashion for avatars in the future. It allows designers to visualize their creations, experiment with different fabrics and colors, and showcase their collections in a digital format. While there are challenges in achieving realism and accuracy, advancements in technology offer new possibilities for designers. Future trends in virtual fashion rendering include real-time rendering, photorealistic rendering, and virtual reality integration, which will further enhance the virtual fashion experience.

5 Virtual Fashion Marketing

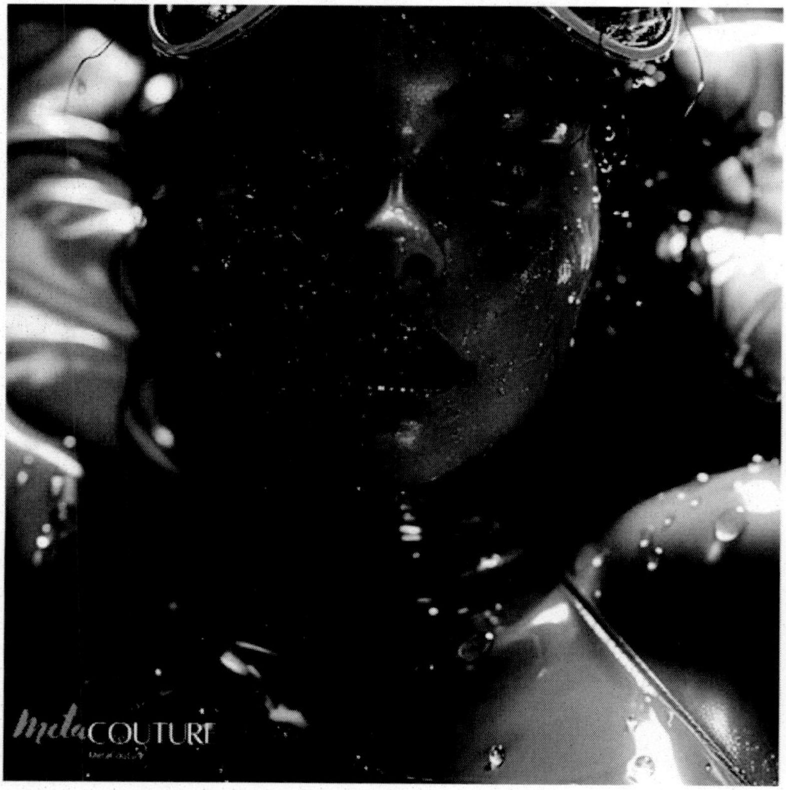

5.1 The Role of Social Media

Social media has become an integral part of our lives, influencing various aspects including fashion. In the world of virtual fashion, social media plays a crucial role in shaping trends, connecting designers with their audience, and promoting virtual fashion brands. This chapter explores the significant role of social media in the virtual fashion industry and how it has revolutionized the way fashion is marketed and consumed.

5.1.1 Building a Virtual Fashion Community

Social media platforms have provided a space for virtual fashion enthusiasts to come together, share their creations, and connect with like-minded individuals. These platforms have created a sense of community where people can express their creativity, seek inspiration, and collaborate with others. Virtual fashion designers can leverage this community to showcase their work, gain feedback, and build a loyal following.

5.1.2 Influencer Marketing in Virtual Fashion

Influencer marketing has become a powerful tool in promoting products and brands, and virtual fashion is no exception. Virtual fashion influencers, who have a significant following on social media platforms, can greatly impact the popularity and success of a virtual fashion brand. These influencers can showcase the latest virtual fashion trends, provide styling tips, and endorse specific brands or designers. Collaborating with virtual fashion influencers can help designers reach a wider audience and increase brand visibility.

5.1.3 Engaging with the Audience

Social media platforms allow designers to directly engage with their audience, creating a more personalized and interactive experience. Designers can share behind-the-scenes glimpses of their creative process, conduct live Q&A sessions, and seek feedback from their followers. This direct interaction not only helps designers understand their audience's preferences but also fosters a sense of connection and loyalty.

5.1.4 Trend Spotting and Market Research

Social media platforms are a treasure trove of information when it comes to spotting emerging trends and conducting market research. Designers can analyze the engagement and response to different virtual fashion styles, colors, and designs to understand what resonates with their target audience. This valuable data can inform their design decisions and help them stay ahead of the curve.

5.1.5 Collaborative Design and Co-Creation

Social media platforms provide a platform for designers to collaborate with other creatives and co-create virtual fashion collections. Designers can connect with virtual stylists, photographers, and models to bring their vision to life. By leveraging the power of social media, designers can find like-minded individuals who share their passion for virtual fashion and work together to create unique and innovative designs.

5.1.6 Viral Marketing and Brand Exposure

The viral nature of social media can catapult a virtual fashion brand into the spotlight. A well-executed marketing campaign or a visually stunning design can quickly gain traction and be shared across various social media platforms. This exposure can lead to increased brand awareness, attract new customers, and establish the brand as a trendsetter in the virtual fashion industry.

5.1.7 Real-Time Feedback and Iteration

Social media platforms enable designers to receive real-time feedback on their designs, allowing them to iterate and improve their creations. By sharing their work-in-progress or conducting polls, designers can involve their audience in the design process and make them feel like valued contributors. This iterative approach not only enhances the quality of the designs but also fosters a sense of inclusivity and co-creation.

5.1.8 Virtual Fashion Events and Shows

Social media has transformed the way virtual fashion events and shows are conducted. Designers can now livestream their fashion shows, allowing a global audience to experience the event in real-time. Social media platforms also enable designers to create virtual fashion events, where attendees can virtually explore collections, interact with avatars, and even make purchases. This virtualization of fashion events opens up new possibilities for designers to showcase their work and reach a wider audience.

5.1.9 Influencing Consumer Behavior

Social media platforms have a significant influence on consumer behavior, shaping their preferences and purchase decisions. Virtual fashion designers can leverage this influence by creating visually appealing content, collaborating with influencers, and engaging with their audience. By strategically utilizing social media, designers can create a desire for their virtual fashion products and drive sales.

In conclusion, social media has revolutionized the virtual fashion industry, providing designers with a powerful platform to connect with their audience, promote their brands, and shape trends. By understanding the role of social media and effectively utilizing its features, virtual fashion designers can establish their presence, build a loyal following, and thrive in the ever-evolving world of virtual fashion.

5.2 Virtual Fashion Influencers

In the world of virtual fashion, influencers play a crucial role in shaping trends, promoting brands, and driving consumer behavior. These virtual fashion influencers are digital avatars who have gained a significant following and influence within the virtual fashion community. They have the power to inspire and guide the fashion choices of millions of virtual fashion enthusiasts.

5.2.1 The Rise of Virtual Fashion Influencers

With the increasing popularity of virtual fashion, the demand for virtual fashion influencers has skyrocketed. These influencers are not limited by physical constraints and can experiment with unique and extravagant styles that may not be possible in the real world. They have the ability to create stunning visuals and showcase the latest virtual fashion designs to their followers.

Virtual fashion influencers have emerged from various platforms, including social media, virtual reality experiences, and online gaming communities. They have built their reputation by consistently creating high-quality content, engaging with their audience, and collaborating with virtual fashion brands.

5.2.2 The Impact of Virtual Fashion Influencers

Virtual fashion influencers have a significant impact on the virtual fashion industry. They have the ability to shape trends, influence purchasing decisions, and drive brand awareness. Their followers look up to them for fashion inspiration, seeking guidance on the latest virtual fashion styles, brands, and accessories.

These influencers collaborate with virtual fashion designers and brands to create exclusive collections, virtual fashion shows, and promotional campaigns. Their endorsements and recommendations carry weight and can significantly boost the visibility and sales of virtual fashion products.

5.2.3 Building a Virtual Fashion Influencer Brand

Becoming a virtual fashion influencer requires a combination of creativity, dedication, and strategic planning. Here are some key steps to building a successful virtual fashion influencer brand:

5.2.3.1 Define Your Style and Niche

To stand out in the virtual fashion influencer space, it's essential to define your unique style and niche. Determine the type of virtual fashion you want to focus on, whether it's futuristic, fantasy, streetwear, or a combination of different styles. Developing a distinct aesthetic will help you attract a dedicated following who resonate with your fashion choices.

5.2.3.2 Create High-Quality Content

Creating high-quality content is crucial for virtual fashion influencers. Invest in high-resolution graphics, animations, and videos to showcase your virtual fashion looks. Experiment with different poses, angles, and lighting techniques to create visually stunning content that captures the attention of your audience.

5.2.3.3 Engage with Your Audience

Engagement is key to building a loyal following. Respond to comments, messages, and inquiries from your audience. Host live streams, Q&A sessions, and virtual fashion tutorials to interact with your followers and provide them with valuable insights and tips.

5.2.3.4 Collaborate with Virtual Fashion Brands

Collaborating with virtual fashion brands is an excellent way to expand your reach and establish credibility. Reach out to virtual fashion designers and brands that align with your style and values. Offer to showcase their designs in your content or collaborate on exclusive collections. These partnerships can help you gain exposure and attract new followers.

5.2.3.5 Stay Up-to-Date with Virtual Fashion Trends

To remain relevant as a virtual fashion influencer, it's crucial to stay up-to-date with the latest trends and developments in the virtual fashion industry. Follow other virtual fashion influencers, attend virtual fashion shows, and participate in virtual fashion communities to stay informed and inspired.

5.2.4 The Future of Virtual Fashion Influencers

As virtual fashion continues to evolve, so will the role of virtual fashion influencers. Here are some potential trends and developments to watch out for:

5.2.4.1 Virtual Fashion Influencer Agencies

With the increasing demand for virtual fashion influencers, specialized agencies may emerge to represent and manage these influencers. These agencies would connect virtual fashion influencers with brands, negotiate partnerships, and provide support and guidance to help influencers grow their brand.

5.2.4.2 Virtual Fashion Influencer Events

Virtual fashion influencer events could become a prominent feature in the virtual fashion industry. These events would bring together virtual fashion influencers, brands, and enthusiasts to showcase the latest virtual fashion trends, collaborate on projects, and network with industry professionals.

5.2.4.3 Virtual Fashion Influencer Merchandise

Virtual fashion influencers may start launching their own merchandise lines, including virtual clothing, accessories, and virtual fashion-related products. This would allow influencers to monetize their brand and provide their followers with exclusive virtual fashion items.

5.2.4.4 Virtual Fashion Influencer Education and Training

As the virtual fashion industry grows, there may be a demand for education and training programs specifically tailored for aspiring virtual fashion influencers. These programs would provide guidance on content creation, brand building, and effective engagement strategies.

In conclusion, virtual fashion influencers have become a powerful force in shaping the virtual fashion industry. Their ability to inspire, guide, and collaborate with virtual fashion brands has made them indispensable in the virtual fashion ecosystem. By understanding the impact of virtual fashion influencers and following the steps to build a successful influencer brand, aspiring virtual fashion enthusiasts can make their mark in this exciting and rapidly evolving industry.

5.3 Virtual Fashion Advertising

In the world of virtual fashion, advertising plays a crucial role in promoting brands, products, and services to a global audience. With the rise of virtual reality (VR) and augmented reality (AR), fashion advertising has taken on a whole new dimension, allowing brands to engage with consumers in immersive and interactive ways. In this section, we will explore the various strategies and techniques used in virtual fashion advertising and how designers can leverage these tools to create impactful campaigns.

5.3.1 The Power of Virtual Fashion Advertising

Virtual fashion advertising offers unique opportunities for brands to showcase their products and connect with consumers in innovative ways. With the ability to create virtual environments and scenarios, brands can transport users into a world where they can experience fashion in a whole new light. Whether it's a virtual runway show, a 360-degree product display, or an interactive shopping experience, virtual fashion advertising allows brands to engage with consumers on a deeper level, creating memorable and immersive experiences.

One of the key advantages of virtual fashion advertising is the ability to reach a global audience. With the internet and social media platforms, brands can easily share their virtual fashion campaigns with people from all corners of the world. This opens up new markets and opportunities for designers to expand their reach and connect with consumers who may not have access to physical stores or fashion events.

5.3.2 Creating Compelling Virtual Fashion Ads

To create compelling virtual fashion ads, designers need to consider the unique characteristics of the virtual environment and the preferences of their target audience. Here are some key strategies to keep in mind:

5.3.2.1 Storytelling

Storytelling is a powerful tool in virtual fashion advertising. By creating narratives around their products or brand, designers can captivate the audience and evoke emotions. Whether it's a story about the inspiration behind a collection or a narrative that transports users into a virtual fashion world, storytelling adds depth and meaning to virtual fashion ads.

5.3.2.2 Interactivity

Interactivity is a key element of virtual fashion advertising. By allowing users to engage with the ad, designers can create a more immersive and memorable experience. This can be achieved through interactive product displays, virtual try-on experiences, or even gamified elements that encourage user participation.

5.3.2.3 Personalization

Personalization is another important aspect of virtual fashion advertising. By tailoring the ad experience to the individual user, designers can create a more personalized and relevant message. This can be done through targeted ads based on user preferences or by allowing users to customize their virtual fashion experience.

5.3.2.4 Collaboration with Influencers

Collaborating with virtual fashion influencers can greatly enhance the reach and impact of advertising campaigns. Influencers have a dedicated following and can help promote brands and products to their audience. By partnering with influencers who align with their brand values, designers can tap into their influence and credibility to reach a wider audience.

5.3.3 Virtual Fashion Advertising Platforms

There are several platforms and technologies available for designers to showcase their virtual fashion ads. Here are some popular options:

5.3.3.1 Social Media Platforms

Social media platforms like Instagram, Facebook, and Snapchat offer a wide range of advertising options for virtual fashion. These platforms allow designers to target specific demographics, create engaging content, and track the performance of their ads. With the ability to share images, videos, and interactive content, social media platforms provide a powerful medium for virtual fashion advertising.

5.3.3.2 Virtual Reality Experiences

Virtual reality experiences provide an immersive platform for virtual fashion advertising. Brands can create virtual fashion shows, interactive shopping experiences, or even virtual showrooms where users can explore and interact with products. Virtual reality headsets like Oculus Rift and HTC Vive offer a high-quality and immersive experience for users, allowing them to fully engage with virtual fashion ads.

5.3.3.3 Augmented Reality Apps

Augmented reality apps allow users to overlay virtual fashion items onto their real-world environment. Brands can create AR experiences where users can try on virtual clothes, accessories, or even experiment with different makeup looks. AR apps like Snapchat's Lens Studio and Apple's ARKit provide designers with the tools to create engaging and interactive virtual fashion ads.

5.3.4 Measuring the Success of Virtual Fashion Ads

Measuring the success of virtual fashion ads is essential to understand the impact of advertising campaigns and make informed decisions for future strategies. Here are some key metrics to consider:

5.3.4.1 Engagement Metrics

Engagement metrics measure how users interact with virtual fashion ads. This includes metrics like click-through rates, time spent on the ad, and interactions such as likes, comments, and shares. By analyzing these metrics, designers can gauge the level of user engagement and identify areas for improvement.

5.3.4.2 Conversion Metrics

Conversion metrics measure the effectiveness of virtual fashion ads in driving desired actions, such as making a purchase or signing up for a newsletter. By tracking conversion rates and analyzing user behavior, designers can optimize their ads to maximize conversions and achieve their advertising goals.

5.3.4.3 Brand Awareness Metrics

Brand awareness metrics measure the impact of virtual fashion ads on brand recognition and recall. This includes metrics like reach, impressions, and brand mentions. By monitoring brand awareness metrics, designers can assess the effectiveness of their advertising campaigns in increasing brand visibility and awareness.

5.3.5 Ethical Considerations in Virtual Fashion Advertising

As with any form of advertising, virtual fashion advertising comes with ethical considerations. Designers need to ensure that their ads are truthful, transparent, and respectful of user privacy. It is important to disclose any virtual enhancements or modifications made to the fashion items and to obtain proper consent from users when collecting their personal data. By adhering to ethical guidelines, designers can build trust with their audience and create a positive brand image.

In conclusion, virtual fashion advertising offers exciting possibilities for designers to showcase their creations and connect with a global audience. By leveraging storytelling, interactivity, personalization, and collaborations with influencers, designers can create compelling virtual fashion ads that leave a lasting impression. With the right platforms and measurement tools, designers can track the success of their ads and make data-driven decisions for future campaigns. It is important to approach virtual fashion advertising ethically, ensuring transparency and respect for user privacy. As the virtual fashion industry continues to evolve, designers who embrace virtual fashion advertising will be well-positioned to thrive in this futuristic landscape.

5.4 Virtual Fashion E-commerce

In the world of virtual fashion, e-commerce plays a crucial role in connecting designers with consumers. Virtual fashion e-commerce platforms provide a convenient and accessible way for people to explore and purchase virtual clothing and accessories for their avatars. This section will delve into the various aspects of virtual fashion e-commerce and how designers can leverage this platform to reach a wider audience and thrive in the digital fashion industry.

5.4.1 The Rise of Virtual Fashion E-commerce

Virtual fashion e-commerce has witnessed a significant rise in popularity in recent years. As more people engage with virtual worlds and create personalized avatars, the demand for virtual fashion has grown exponentially. Virtual fashion e-commerce platforms have emerged as the go-to destinations for users to discover and purchase virtual clothing items, accessories, and even virtual beauty products.

These platforms provide a seamless shopping experience, allowing users to browse through a wide range of virtual fashion items, try them on their avatars, and make purchases with just a few clicks. Virtual fashion e-commerce has not only revolutionized the way people shop for virtual clothing but has also opened up new opportunities for designers to showcase their creations and monetize their talent.

5.4.2 Designing for Virtual Fashion E-commerce

Designing for virtual fashion e-commerce requires a unique approach compared to traditional fashion design. While the principles of design remain the same, there are a few key considerations that designers need to keep in mind to create successful virtual fashion collections for e-commerce platforms.

5.4.2.1 Avatar Compatibility

One of the primary considerations when designing for virtual fashion e-commerce is avatar compatibility. Designers must ensure that their clothing items are compatible with a wide range of avatar body types and shapes. This requires creating clothing that can adapt and fit seamlessly onto different avatars, regardless of their size or proportions. By offering a diverse range of sizes and customization options, designers can cater to a broader audience and enhance the inclusivity of their virtual fashion brand.

5.4.2.2 Virtual Fabric Realism

In virtual fashion e-commerce, the visual appeal of clothing plays a crucial role in attracting customers. Designers must focus on creating virtual fabrics that are visually appealing and realistic. This involves paying attention to details such as texture, shine, and drape to mimic real-world fabrics. By using advanced rendering techniques and 3D modeling, designers can create virtual fabrics that closely resemble their real-world counterparts, enhancing the overall shopping experience for users.

5.4.2.3 Interactive Try-On Features

One of the advantages of virtual fashion e-commerce is the ability for users to try on clothing items virtually before making a purchase. Designers can enhance the user experience by incorporating interactive try-on features into their e-commerce platforms. These features allow users to see how a particular clothing item would look on their avatar in real-time, enabling them to make more informed purchasing decisions. By providing this interactive element, designers can increase user engagement and boost sales.

5.4.2.4 Customization Options

Virtual fashion e-commerce platforms often provide users with the option to customize their clothing items. Designers can leverage this feature by offering a range of customization options, such as color variations, patterns, and embellishments. By allowing users to personalize their virtual clothing, designers can create a sense of exclusivity and uniqueness, making their products more desirable to consumers.

5.4.3 Marketing and Promoting Virtual Fashion E-commerce

To succeed in the virtual fashion e-commerce industry, designers must effectively market and promote their virtual fashion collections. Here are some strategies that designers can employ to increase visibility and drive sales:

5.4.3.1 Social Media Marketing

Social media platforms play a crucial role in promoting virtual fashion e-commerce. Designers can leverage platforms like Instagram, Facebook, and TikTok to showcase their virtual fashion collections, engage with their target audience, and build a strong online presence. By collaborating with virtual fashion influencers and utilizing targeted advertising, designers can reach a wider audience and generate interest in their virtual fashion brand.

5.4.3.2 Virtual Fashion Events and Shows

Virtual fashion events and shows provide an excellent opportunity for designers to showcase their collections and generate buzz around their brand. By participating in virtual fashion weeks or organizing their own virtual fashion shows, designers can attract attention from industry professionals, media, and potential customers. These events can be live-streamed or pre-recorded, allowing users from around the world to experience the excitement of a fashion show from the comfort of their own homes.

5.4.3.3 Collaborations and Partnerships

Collaborating with other virtual fashion designers, brands, or influencers can be a powerful marketing strategy. By partnering with like-minded individuals or organizations, designers can tap into their existing audience and gain exposure to new potential customers. Collaborations can take the form of joint virtual fashion collections, co-branded marketing campaigns, or even virtual fashion competitions. These partnerships can help designers expand their reach and establish themselves as key players in the virtual fashion industry.

5.4.4 The Future of Virtual Fashion E-commerce

The future of virtual fashion e-commerce looks promising, with advancements in technology and increasing consumer interest in virtual experiences. As virtual reality and augmented reality technologies continue to evolve, designers can expect more immersive and interactive virtual fashion e-commerce platforms. Virtual fashion shows and events may become more commonplace, allowing users to virtually attend and participate in the fashion industry from anywhere in the world.

Furthermore, the integration of artificial intelligence and machine learning algorithms can enhance the personalization and recommendation features of virtual fashion e-commerce platforms. By analyzing user preferences and behavior, these algorithms can suggest clothing items that align with individual tastes, making the shopping experience more tailored and enjoyable.

In conclusion, virtual fashion e-commerce presents a world of opportunities for designers to showcase their creativity and connect with a global audience. By understanding the unique aspects of designing for virtual fashion e-commerce and implementing effective marketing strategies, designers can thrive in this rapidly evolving industry. As technology continues to advance, virtual fashion e-commerce is poised to become an integral part of the fashion industry, offering endless possibilities for designers and consumers alike.

6 Virtual Fashion Sustainability

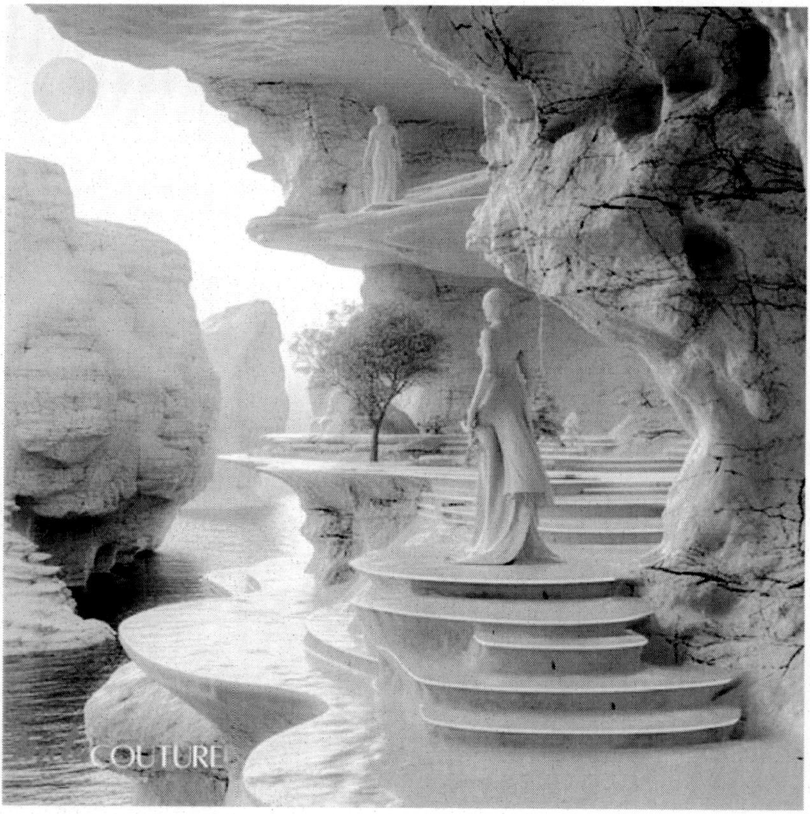

6.1 Environmental Impact of Virtual Fashion

As the fashion industry continues to evolve, so does the concept of virtual fashion. Virtual fashion offers a unique and innovative approach to clothing design, allowing individuals to express their style and creativity in a virtual world. While virtual fashion has many advantages, it is important to consider its environmental impact.

6.1.1 Sustainable Materials in Virtual Fashion

One of the keyways to reduce the environmental impact of virtual fashion is through the use of sustainable materials. Just like in traditional fashion, the choice of materials in virtual fashion plays a crucial role in its sustainability. Designers can opt for virtual fabrics that are made from recycled or upcycled materials, reducing the need for new resources.

Virtual fashion also provides an opportunity to experiment with materials that are not feasible in the physical world. For example, designers can create virtual fabrics that mimic the appearance and texture of exotic materials like fur or leather, without the need for animal products. This not only reduces the environmental impact but also promotes ethical fashion practices.

6.1.2 Reduced Waste and Energy Consumption

Another significant advantage of virtual fashion is the reduction in waste and energy consumption. In traditional fashion, the production process often leads to a significant amount of waste, from fabric scraps to unsold inventory. Virtual fashion eliminates the need for physical production, resulting in minimal waste generation.

Additionally, virtual fashion reduces energy consumption associated with manufacturing, transportation, and storage. Virtual garments are created and displayed digitally, eliminating the need for physical transportation and storage facilities. This not only reduces carbon emissions but also conserves energy resources.

6.1.3 Decreased Water Usage

Water scarcity is a pressing issue in many parts of the world, and the fashion industry is known to be a major contributor to water pollution and wastage. Virtual fashion offers a solution to this problem by significantly reducing water usage. Unlike traditional fashion, virtual fashion does not require water-intensive processes such as dyeing, washing, and finishing.

By eliminating the need for water-intensive processes, virtual fashion helps conserve this precious resource and reduces the pollution caused by the discharge of chemicals into water bodies. This makes virtual fashion a more sustainable alternative, especially in regions where water scarcity is a concern.

6.1.4 Lower Carbon Footprint

The carbon footprint of the fashion industry is a significant contributor to climate change. From the production of raw materials to the transportation of finished products, traditional fashion has a substantial carbon footprint. Virtual fashion, on the other hand, has the potential to significantly reduce carbon emissions.

By eliminating the need for physical production and transportation, virtual fashion reduces the carbon emissions associated with the fashion supply chain. Additionally, the use of sustainable materials and reduced energy consumption further contributes to lowering the carbon footprint of virtual fashion.

6.1.5 Challenges and Considerations

While virtual fashion offers numerous environmental benefits, it is important to consider the challenges and limitations associated with its implementation. One of the key challenges is the reliance on technology and energy-intensive infrastructure. The production and maintenance of the required hardware and software can have its own environmental impact.

Another consideration is the disposal of virtual garments. As virtual fashion evolves, there may be a need to update or replace virtual garments, which could result in electronic waste. It is crucial to develop sustainable practices for the disposal and recycling of virtual fashion items to minimize their environmental impact.

6.1.6 The Future of Sustainable Virtual Fashion

As the fashion industry continues to embrace virtual fashion, there is a growing focus on sustainability. Designers and technologists are exploring innovative ways to further reduce the environmental impact of virtual fashion. This includes the development of more sustainable materials, energy-efficient technologies, and responsible disposal practices.

Collaboration between fashion designers, technologists, and environmental experts is essential to drive the development of sustainable virtual fashion. By working together, they can create a future where virtual fashion not only offers endless creative possibilities but also contributes to a more sustainable and environmentally conscious industry.

In conclusion, virtual fashion has the potential to significantly reduce the environmental impact of the fashion industry. Through the use of sustainable materials, reduced waste and energy consumption, decreased water usage, and lower carbon footprint, virtual fashion offers a more sustainable alternative to traditional fashion. However, it is important to address the challenges and considerations associated with virtual fashion to ensure its long-term sustainability. By embracing sustainable practices and fostering collaboration, the future of virtual fashion can be both fashionable and environmentally responsible.

6.2 Sustainable Virtual Fabrication

As the fashion industry continues to evolve, sustainability has become a crucial consideration in every aspect of the design process. This includes virtual fashion, where the concept of sustainable virtual fabrication is gaining traction. Sustainable virtual fabrication refers to the use of environmentally friendly and ethical practices in the creation of virtual fashion garments and accessories. In this section, we will explore the importance of sustainable virtual fabrication and discuss various strategies that can be employed to achieve it.

6.2.1 The Need for Sustainable Virtual Fabrication

The fashion industry has long been criticized for its negative impact on the environment. From the excessive use of natural resources to the pollution caused by textile production, traditional fashion practices have contributed to significant environmental degradation. With the rise of virtual fashion, there is an opportunity to address these issues and create a more sustainable future for the industry.

Sustainable virtual fabrication offers several advantages over traditional fashion production methods. Firstly, it eliminates the need for physical materials, reducing the consumption of resources such as water, energy, and raw materials. By designing and creating virtual garments, designers can minimize waste and reduce their carbon footprint.

Secondly, sustainable virtual fabrication allows for greater flexibility and experimentation in the design process. Designers can easily modify and iterate their creations without the limitations imposed by physical materials. This encourages innovation and creativity, leading to the development of unique and sustainable virtual fashion pieces.

Lastly, sustainable virtual fabrication promotes ethical practices in the fashion industry. By eliminating the need for physical production, designers can avoid the exploitation of labor and ensure fair working conditions. This ethical approach extends to the entire supply chain, from the creation of virtual fabrics to the virtual fashion shows and marketing campaigns.

6.2.2 Strategies for Sustainable Virtual Fabrication

To achieve sustainable virtual fabrication, designers can adopt various strategies that prioritize environmental and ethical considerations. Here are some key approaches to consider:

6.2.2.1 Virtual Fabric Selection

Choosing sustainable virtual fabrics is a crucial step in the design process. Designers can opt for virtual fabrics that mimic the properties of real-world sustainable materials, such as organic cotton, bamboo, or recycled polyester. By using these virtual fabrics, designers can create garments that have a lower environmental impact and promote sustainable practices.

6.2.2.2 Virtual Supply Chain Management

Managing the virtual supply chain is another important aspect of sustainable virtual fabrication. Designers should collaborate with virtual fabric manufacturers and suppliers who adhere to sustainable practices. This includes ensuring that the virtual fabric production process is energy-efficient, uses non-toxic dyes, and minimizes waste generation. By partnering with ethical suppliers, designers can ensure that their virtual fashion creations align with sustainable principles.

6.2.2.3 Virtual Production Techniques

In virtual fashion, designers have the freedom to experiment with innovative production techniques that minimize waste and resource consumption. For example, virtual garments can be designed to be modular, allowing for easy customization and reconfiguration. This reduces the need for creating entirely new garments and promotes a circular economy approach to fashion.

6.2.2.4 Virtual Recycling and Upcycling

Just like in the physical fashion industry, virtual fashion can also embrace recycling and upcycling practices. Designers can repurpose existing virtual garments and accessories, giving them new life and reducing the demand for new creations. This approach not only reduces waste but also encourages sustainable consumption patterns among virtual fashion enthusiasts.

6.2.2.5 Education and Awareness

Promoting education and awareness about sustainable virtual fabrication is crucial for its widespread adoption. Designers, consumers, and industry professionals should be educated about the environmental and ethical benefits of virtual fashion. This can be done through workshops, seminars, and online resources that highlight the importance of sustainable practices in virtual fashion.

6.2.3 The Future of Sustainable Virtual Fabrication

The future of sustainable virtual fabrication looks promising. As technology continues to advance, designers will have access to more sophisticated tools and software that enable them to create virtual fashion with even greater precision and realism. This will further enhance the potential for sustainable virtual fabrication by allowing designers to simulate the environmental impact of their virtual creations and make informed decisions about materials and production techniques.

Furthermore, as consumer demand for sustainable fashion grows, virtual fashion has the potential to become a viable alternative to physical fashion. Virtual fashion offers the opportunity for consumers to express their style and creativity without contributing to the environmental and ethical issues associated with traditional fashion. This shift towards sustainable virtual fabrication has the potential to revolutionize the industry and pave the way for a more sustainable and ethical future.

In conclusion, sustainable virtual fabrication is a crucial aspect of the future of fashion. By adopting environmentally friendly and ethical practices in the creation of virtual fashion, designers can minimize their impact on the environment and promote a more sustainable industry. Through the careful selection of virtual fabrics, responsible supply chain management, innovative production techniques, and a focus on recycling and upcycling, sustainable virtual fabrication can become the norm in the virtual fashion world. It is up to designers, consumers, and industry professionals to embrace this shift and work towards a more sustainable and ethical future for fashion.

6.3 Ethical Considerations in Virtual Fashion

As the world of fashion continues to evolve, virtual fashion has emerged as a powerful and innovative trend. With the rise of virtual reality and augmented reality technologies, designers now have the ability to create stunning couture fashion for avatars in virtual environments. However, as with any new technology, there are ethical considerations that need to be taken into account.

6.3.1 Body Image and Unrealistic Standards

One of the primary ethical concerns in virtual fashion is the perpetuation of unrealistic body standards. In the virtual world, designers have the freedom to create avatars with idealized proportions and flawless features. While this may be seen as an artistic expression, it can also contribute to body image issues and low self-esteem among individuals who do not fit these standards.

To address this concern, it is important for designers to promote diversity and inclusivity in their virtual fashion creations. By designing avatars that represent a wide range of body types, ethnicities, and ages, designers can help to challenge the narrow beauty standards that have long been prevalent in the fashion industry. Additionally, designers should consider incorporating customizable features that allow users to personalize their avatars to better reflect their own unique identities.

6.3.2 Cultural Appropriation

Another ethical consideration in virtual fashion is the potential for cultural appropriation. With the ability to create avatars inspired by different cultures, there is a risk of misrepresentation and disrespect. Designers must be mindful of the cultural significance of certain garments, symbols, and patterns, and ensure that they are used in a respectful and informed manner.

To avoid cultural appropriation, designers should engage in thorough research and consultation with individuals from the cultures they are drawing inspiration from. This includes understanding the historical and cultural context of the garments and seeking permission or collaboration with artists and artisans from those cultures. By doing so, designers can create virtual fashion that celebrates and respects diverse cultures without appropriating or misrepresenting them.

6.3.3 Sustainability and Virtual Waste

While virtual fashion offers the potential for reducing the environmental impact of the fashion industry, there are still ethical considerations when it comes to sustainability. Virtual fashion may not produce physical waste like traditional fashion, but it still requires energy and resources to create and maintain virtual environments.

Designers should strive to minimize the carbon footprint of virtual fashion by using renewable energy sources and optimizing the efficiency of virtual fashion platforms. Additionally, they should consider the lifespan of virtual fashion creations and avoid creating disposable virtual garments that contribute to virtual waste. By promoting sustainable practices in virtual fashion, designers can help to mitigate the environmental impact of the industry.

6.3.4 Intellectual Property and Copyright

With the ease of digital reproduction and distribution in virtual environments, intellectual property and copyright issues become significant ethical considerations. Designers must be aware of the legal implications of using copyrighted materials, such as logos, patterns, and designs, in their virtual fashion creations.

To ensure ethical practices, designers should obtain proper permissions and licenses for any copyrighted materials they use. They should also respect the intellectual property rights of other designers and artists, avoiding plagiarism and unauthorized use of their work. By upholding intellectual property rights, designers can foster a culture of creativity and innovation in the virtual fashion industry.

6.3.5 Data Privacy and Security

In the virtual fashion industry, data privacy and security are crucial ethical considerations. Virtual fashion platforms collect and store user data, including personal information and preferences. Designers and platform operators must prioritize the protection of this data and ensure that it is used responsibly and ethically.

To address data privacy concerns, designers should implement robust security measures to safeguard user data from unauthorized access or breaches. They should also be transparent about their data collection and usage practices, providing users with clear information and options for consent. By prioritizing data privacy and security, designers can build trust with their users and maintain ethical standards in the virtual fashion industry.

In conclusion, while virtual fashion opens up exciting possibilities for creativity and innovation, it is important to consider the ethical implications of this emerging trend. By promoting diversity, inclusivity, and sustainability, designers can create virtual fashion that is not only visually stunning but also socially responsible. By addressing ethical considerations such as body image, cultural appropriation, sustainability, intellectual property, and data privacy, the virtual fashion industry can thrive while upholding ethical standards.

6.4 Virtual Fashion Recycling and Upcycling

As the fashion industry continues to evolve and embrace virtual fashion, it is essential to consider the environmental impact of this digital realm. Virtual fashion offers a unique opportunity to explore sustainable practices, including recycling and upcycling, in order to minimize waste and reduce the industry's carbon footprint. In this section, we will delve into the concept of virtual fashion recycling and upcycling and explore how designers can incorporate these practices into their virtual couture creations.

6.4.1 The Importance of Virtual Fashion Recycling

Just like in the physical world, virtual fashion also generates waste. As avatars change their outfits and fashion trends evolve, there is a need to address the disposal of virtual garments. Virtual fashion recycling involves the process of reusing or repurposing digital clothing items to extend their lifespan and reduce the need for constant production of new designs. By implementing recycling practices in the virtual fashion industry, designers can contribute to a more sustainable and eco-friendly future.

6.4.2 Upcycling in Virtual Fashion

Upcycling is a creative and innovative approach to sustainability that involves transforming old or discarded materials into new and improved products. In the context of virtual fashion, upcycling can be applied by repurposing existing digital garments or elements to create unique and original designs. Designers can experiment with combining different virtual fabrics, textures, and patterns to breathe new life into outdated or unused virtual clothing items. This not only reduces waste but also adds a sense of individuality and exclusivity to the virtual fashion landscape.

6.4.3 Virtual Fashion Recycling Techniques

To effectively implement virtual fashion recycling and upcycling, designers can employ various techniques and strategies. Here are a few examples:

6.4.3.1 Virtual Garment Swapping

Virtual garment swapping platforms can be created to facilitate the exchange of digital clothing items between avatars. This allows users to refresh their virtual wardrobe without the need for constant production of new designs. By encouraging the reuse of virtual garments, designers can significantly reduce the environmental impact of virtual fashion.

6.4.3.2 Virtual Fashion Rental Services

Similar to physical fashion rental services, virtual fashion rental platforms can be established to provide avatars with access to a wide range of virtual garments for a limited period. This not only promotes the reuse of digital clothing but also allows users to experiment with different styles and trends without the need for permanent ownership.

6.4.3.3 Virtual Fashion Resale Marketplaces

Virtual fashion resale marketplaces can be created to enable avatars to sell or trade their pre-owned digital clothing items. This not only extends the lifespan of virtual garments but also provides an opportunity for users to earn virtual currency or rewards by participating in the circular economy of virtual fashion.

6.4.3.4 Virtual Fashion Customization

Designers can encourage users to customize their virtual garments by providing tools and options for altering the design, color, or texture of existing digital clothing items. This allows avatars to personalize their outfits and breathe new life into old designs, reducing the need for constant production of new virtual garments.

6.4.4 Benefits of Virtual Fashion Recycling and Upcycling

The incorporation of virtual fashion recycling and upcycling practices brings several benefits to both the environment and the fashion industry as a whole:

6.4.4.1 Reduced Waste and Carbon Footprint

By reusing and repurposing virtual garments, designers can significantly reduce the amount of waste generated in the virtual fashion industry. This, in turn, helps to minimize the carbon footprint associated with the production and disposal of digital clothing items.

6.4.4.2 Increased Sustainability

Virtual fashion recycling and upcycling contribute to a more sustainable fashion industry by promoting the efficient use of resources and reducing the reliance on constant production of new designs. This shift towards a circular economy in virtual fashion aligns with the principles of sustainability and responsible consumption.

6.4.4.3 Enhanced Creativity and Innovation

The practice of upcycling in virtual fashion encourages designers to think outside the box and explore new possibilities. By repurposing existing digital garments, designers can create unique and original designs that showcase their creativity and innovation.

6.4.4.4 Consumer Engagement and Satisfaction

Virtual fashion recycling and upcycling initiatives provide users with a sense of engagement and participation in the sustainability efforts of the fashion industry. By offering platforms for garment swapping, rental services, and resale marketplaces, designers can foster a sense of community and satisfaction among virtual fashion enthusiasts.

In conclusion, virtual fashion recycling and upcycling are crucial aspects of sustainable virtual fashion design. By implementing these practices, designers can contribute to reducing waste, minimizing the carbon footprint, and promoting a circular economy in the virtual fashion industry. Through virtual garment swapping, rental services, resale marketplaces, and customization options, designers can engage users in the process of sustainability and foster creativity and innovation. Embracing virtual fashion recycling and upcycling not only benefits the environment but also enhances the overall experience and satisfaction of virtual fashion enthusiasts.

7 Virtual Fashion in Entertainment

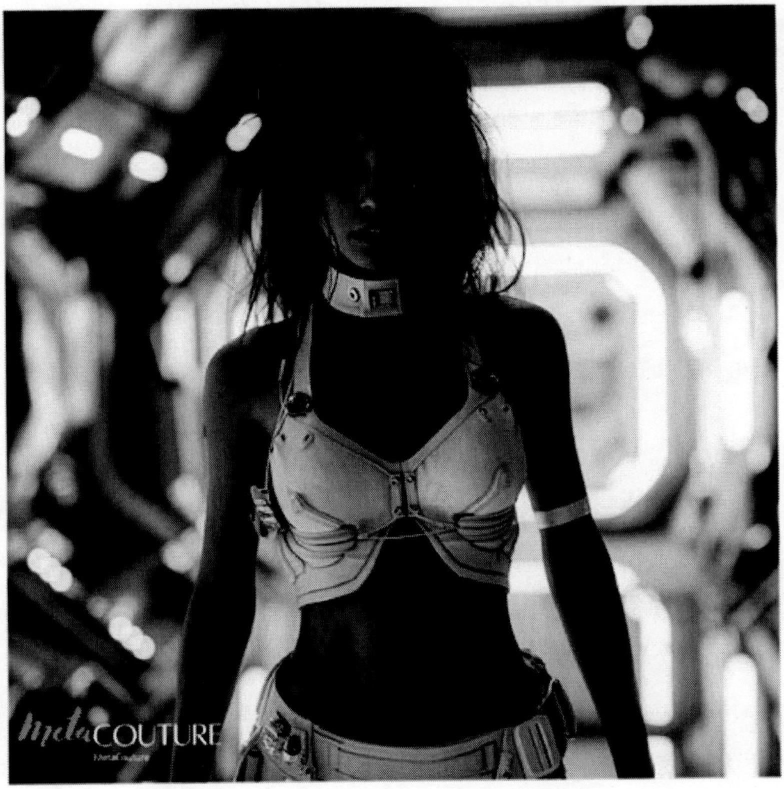

7.1 Virtual Fashion in Movies and TV Shows

Virtual fashion has become an integral part of the entertainment industry, particularly in movies and TV shows. The use of virtual fashion in these mediums allows for limitless creativity and the ability to bring fantastical designs to life. In this section, we will explore the impact of virtual fashion in movies and TV shows and how it has revolutionized the way costumes are designed and presented.

The Evolution of Fashion in Movies and TV Shows

Fashion has always played a significant role in movies and TV shows. From iconic costumes that define characters to the portrayal of different time periods and cultures, fashion has the power to enhance storytelling and create memorable visuals. In the past, costume designers relied on physical garments and accessories to bring their visions to life. However, with the advent of virtual fashion, the possibilities have expanded exponentially.

Advantages of Virtual Fashion in Movies and TV Shows

Virtual fashion offers numerous advantages when it comes to designing costumes for movies and TV shows. One of the primary benefits is the ability to create intricate and elaborate designs that may not be feasible or practical in the physical world. Virtual fashion allows costume designers to push the boundaries of creativity and experiment with unconventional materials, shapes, and textures.

Another advantage of virtual fashion is the ease of customization. With virtual avatars, costume designers can easily modify and adjust garments to fit the specific requirements of each character. This flexibility allows for a more precise and tailored approach to costume design, ensuring that every detail is perfect.

Virtual fashion also offers cost and time-saving benefits. Creating physical garments can be time-consuming and expensive, especially when dealing with complex designs or multiple iterations. With virtual fashion, designers can quickly visualize and iterate on their designs without the need for physical prototypes. This not only saves time but also reduces material waste and production costs.

Virtual Fashion in Costume Design

Virtual fashion has revolutionized the way costumes are designed for movies and TV shows. Costume designers now have access to a vast library of virtual fabrics, textures, and patterns, allowing them to create unique and visually stunning costumes. They can experiment with different combinations and styles, ensuring that each character's costume reflects their personality and role in the story.

Virtual fashion also allows for seamless integration of special effects and CGI. Costume designers can collaborate with visual effects artists to create costumes that seamlessly blend with the virtual environments and characters. This integration enhances the overall visual experience and creates a more immersive world for the audience.

Virtual Fashion in Character Development

Costumes play a crucial role in character development, and virtual fashion offers new opportunities for designers to enhance this aspect. By using virtual avatars, costume designers can create costumes that not only reflect the character's personality but also evolve with their journey. Virtual fashion allows for dynamic and transformative costumes that can change and adapt as the character progresses through the story.

Additionally, virtual fashion enables designers to explore the cultural and historical context of a character's costume more deeply. They can research and incorporate intricate details and traditional elements that may not be readily available in the physical world. This attention to detail adds depth and authenticity to the characters and their costumes.

Virtual Fashion in Visual Storytelling

Virtual fashion has the power to elevate visual storytelling in movies and TV shows. With the ability to create stunning and otherworldly designs, costume designers can enhance the narrative and create memorable visual moments. Whether it's a futuristic sci-fi film or a period drama, virtual fashion allows for the creation of unique and visually striking costumes that captivate the audience's attention.

Furthermore, virtual fashion opens up new possibilities for character expression and communication. Through their costumes, characters can convey their emotions, status, and relationships with other characters. Virtual fashion enables designers to push the boundaries of costume design, creating garments that are not only visually appealing but also serve as storytelling tools.

Conclusion

Virtual fashion has revolutionized the way costumes are designed and presented in movies and TV shows. It offers numerous advantages, including limitless creativity, customization, cost and time savings, and seamless integration with special effects. Virtual fashion allows costume designers to create intricate and elaborate designs, tailor costumes to each character, and enhance visual storytelling. As technology continues to advance, we can expect virtual fashion to play an even more significant role in the entertainment industry, pushing the boundaries of creativity and imagination.

7.2 Virtual Fashion in Video Games

Video games have become a significant platform for virtual fashion, allowing players to express their personal style and creativity through their avatars. The integration of virtual fashion in video games has revolutionized the gaming industry, providing players with endless possibilities to customize their characters' appearance and attire. In this section, we will explore the impact of virtual fashion in video games and how it has transformed the gaming experience.

7.2.1 The Role of Virtual Fashion in Video Games

Virtual fashion plays a crucial role in video games, enhancing the immersive experience for players. It allows gamers to create unique and visually appealing avatars that reflect their individuality and personal taste. The ability to dress up avatars in various virtual outfits and accessories adds depth and realism to the gaming world, making it more engaging and enjoyable.

In many video games, fashion items and customization options are not merely cosmetic but also serve as rewards for completing challenges or progressing through the game. This incentivizes players to explore different aspects of the game and strive for achievements, creating a sense of accomplishment and motivation. Virtual fashion in video games has become a form of self-expression, enabling players to showcase their creativity and style within the virtual realm.

7.2.2 Fashion Design and Collaboration in Video Games

Designing virtual fashion for video games requires a unique set of skills and collaboration between fashion designers and game developers. The process involves creating 3D models of garments, textures, and animations that seamlessly integrate with the game's graphics and mechanics. Collaboration between fashion designers and game developers ensures that the virtual fashion aligns with the game's aesthetics and narrative.

Fashion designers working on virtual fashion for video games must consider the specific requirements of the gaming environment. The garments need to be visually appealing, functional, and able to adapt to the movements and actions of the avatars. Collaboration between fashion designers and game developers allows for the creation of virtual fashion that not only looks good but also enhances the gameplay experience.

7.2.3 Virtual Fashion as a Marketing Tool in Video Games

Virtual fashion has also become a powerful marketing tool within the gaming industry. Many video games offer in-game purchases, allowing players to buy virtual fashion items and accessories using real or in-game currency. This creates a new revenue stream for game developers and fashion brands, as players are willing to invest in virtual fashion to enhance their gaming experience.

Fashion collaborations between video game developers and real-world fashion brands have become increasingly common. These collaborations often involve the integration of real-world fashion collections into the virtual gaming world, allowing players to dress their avatars in the latest fashion trends. This cross-promotion benefits both the fashion brand and the video game, as it expands their reach to new audiences and creates a buzz around their products.

7.2.4 Virtual Fashion and Social Interaction in Video Games

Virtual fashion in video games not only allows players to express their personal style but also facilitates social interaction within the gaming community. Players can showcase their avatars' fashion choices and engage in virtual fashion discussions with other players. This creates a sense of belonging and community, as players bond over their shared interest in virtual fashion.

Some video games even host virtual fashion shows or competitions, where players can showcase their fashion creations and compete for recognition within the gaming community. These events foster creativity, competition, and collaboration among players, further enhancing the social aspect of virtual fashion in video games.

7.2.5 The Future of Virtual Fashion in Video Games

As technology continues to advance, the future of virtual fashion in video games looks promising. With the advent of virtual reality (VR) and augmented reality (AR) technologies, players will have even more immersive and interactive experiences with virtual fashion. VR headsets and AR devices will allow players to see themselves wearing virtual fashion in real-time, blurring the lines between the virtual and physical worlds.

Furthermore, advancements in artificial intelligence (AI) will enable more realistic and dynamic virtual fashion. AI algorithms can analyze players' preferences and behaviors to generate personalized virtual fashion recommendations, making the gaming experience even more tailored to individual players.

In conclusion, virtual fashion in video games has transformed the gaming experience, allowing players to express their personal style and creativity through their avatars. It has become a powerful marketing tool, a means of social interaction, and a platform for collaboration between fashion designers and game developers. As technology continues to evolve, the future of virtual fashion in video games holds exciting possibilities for even more immersive and personalized gaming experiences.

7.3 Virtual Fashion in Virtual Reality Experiences

Virtual reality (VR) has revolutionized the way we experience and interact with the digital world. It has opened up new possibilities in various industries, including fashion. In this chapter, we will explore the exciting realm of virtual fashion in virtual reality experiences.

7.3.1 The Immersive Virtual Fashion Experience

Virtual reality offers a unique opportunity to immerse oneself in a virtual world, where the boundaries of reality are blurred. In the context of fashion, VR allows users to step into a virtual boutique or runway show, where they can explore and interact with virtual garments and accessories. This immersive experience provides a new level of engagement and excitement for fashion enthusiasts.

7.3.2 Virtual Fashion Design in VR

Designing virtual fashion in VR involves a combination of traditional fashion design principles and digital tools. Fashion designers can use VR technology to create and manipulate virtual garments, experimenting with different styles, fabrics, and patterns. They can also collaborate with other designers and artists in real-time, regardless of their physical location.

Virtual reality enables designers to visualize their creations in a three-dimensional space, allowing for a more accurate representation of how the garments will look and move on a virtual avatar. This level of detail and realism enhances the design process and enables designers to make informed decisions about the fit, silhouette, and overall aesthetics of their virtual couture.

7.3.3 Virtual Fashion Shows in VR

Virtual fashion shows have become increasingly popular in recent years, and VR technology has taken these shows to a whole new level. In a virtual fashion show, users can attend from the comfort of their own homes and experience the excitement of a live runway show. They can interact with the virtual models, view the garments from different angles, and even make virtual purchases.

Designers can showcase their virtual couture collections in a virtual environment that reflects their brand identity and aesthetic. They can create stunning virtual sets, lighting effects, and music to enhance the overall experience. Virtual fashion shows also provide an opportunity for designers to reach a global audience, breaking down geographical barriers and expanding their brand presence.

7.3.4 Virtual Fashion Retail in VR

Virtual reality has the potential to revolutionize the way we shop for fashion. In a virtual retail environment, users can browse through virtual boutiques, try on virtual garments, and make purchases without leaving their homes. This eliminates the need for physical stores and allows for a more personalized and convenient shopping experience.

Virtual fashion retail also opens up new possibilities for customization. Users can personalize their avatars and try on different virtual garments to see how they look and fit. They can experiment with different styles and combinations, allowing for a more interactive and exploratory shopping experience.

7.3.5 Virtual Fashion Collaboration in VR

Virtual reality enables designers, artists, and other fashion professionals to collaborate in a virtual space, regardless of their physical location. They can work together in real-time, sharing ideas, sketches, and designs. This level of collaboration fosters creativity and innovation, as different perspectives and expertise can be easily integrated into the design process.

Virtual fashion collaboration also allows for more inclusive and diverse design practices. Designers can collaborate with individuals from different backgrounds and cultures, bringing unique perspectives and experiences to the table. This diversity in collaboration can lead to the creation of more inclusive and representative virtual fashion collections.

7.3.6 The Future of Virtual Fashion in VR

The future of virtual fashion in virtual reality experiences is promising. As VR technology continues to advance, we can expect more realistic and immersive virtual fashion experiences. Virtual reality headsets are becoming more accessible and affordable, making it easier for fashion enthusiasts to engage with virtual fashion.

In the future, we may see virtual fashion becoming an integral part of our everyday lives. Virtual garments and accessories could be seamlessly integrated into our digital identities, allowing us to express ourselves in new and exciting ways. Virtual fashion may also have a positive impact on sustainability, as it reduces the need for physical production and consumption.

To prepare for the future of virtual fashion in VR, fashion designers should embrace new technologies and develop skills in virtual design and collaboration. They should stay updated with the latest advancements in VR technology and explore ways to incorporate virtual fashion into their design processes. By embracing virtual fashion, designers can unlock a world of endless possibilities and shape the future of the fashion industry.

7.4 Virtual Fashion in Music Videos

Music videos have always been a platform for artists to express their creativity and showcase their unique style. In recent years, virtual fashion has become an integral part of music videos, allowing artists to push the boundaries of fashion and create visually stunning experiences. This chapter explores the role of virtual fashion in music videos and how it has revolutionized the way we perceive fashion and music.

7.4.1 The Fusion of Fashion and Music

Music videos have long been a medium for artists to tell a story and convey emotions through visuals. With the advent of virtual fashion, artists now have the opportunity to enhance their storytelling by incorporating futuristic and avant-garde fashion designs into their videos. Virtual fashion allows artists to experiment with bold and unconventional styles that may not be feasible in the physical world.

7.4.2 Creating Unique Visual Identities

Virtual fashion in music videos offers artists the chance to create unique visual identities that align with their music and persona. By collaborating with virtual fashion designers, artists can bring their wildest fashion fantasies to life. From extravagant costumes to surreal outfits, virtual fashion allows artists to fully immerse themselves in a world of limitless possibilities.

7.4.3 Enhancing the Visual Experience

Virtual fashion adds an extra layer of visual appeal to music videos, making them more captivating and memorable. Through the use of advanced technologies such as motion capture and CGI, virtual fashion can seamlessly blend with the artist's movements, creating a mesmerizing visual spectacle. The dynamic and interactive nature of virtual fashion allows artists to engage their audience on a whole new level.

7.4.4 Collaborations between Artists and Designers

Virtual fashion in music videos often involves collaborations between artists and virtual fashion designers. These collaborations bring together the creative minds of both the artist and the designer, resulting in groundbreaking and innovative fashion concepts. By working closely with virtual fashion designers, artists can explore new possibilities and push the boundaries of fashion in music videos.

7.4.5 Showcasing Futuristic Fashion Trends

Music videos have always been a platform for showcasing the latest fashion trends. With virtual fashion, artists can take this to a whole new level by introducing futuristic fashion trends that are yet to be seen in the physical world. From holographic garments to interactive digital accessories, virtual fashion allows artists to set new trends and inspire fashion enthusiasts around the globe.

7.4.6 Creating Immersive Visual Worlds

Virtual fashion in music videos not only transforms the artist's appearance but also creates immersive visual worlds that transport the audience into a different reality. By combining virtual fashion with stunning visual effects and CGI, music videos can transport viewers to futuristic landscapes, surreal environments, and otherworldly realms. This fusion of fashion and technology creates a truly immersive and unforgettable experience.

7.4.7 Pushing the Boundaries of Creativity

Virtual fashion in music videos has opened up a whole new realm of creative possibilities. Artists are no longer limited by the constraints of physical materials and can explore unconventional shapes, textures, and colors. Virtual fashion allows artists to push the boundaries of creativity and create fashion-forward looks that defy traditional norms.

7.4.8 Inspiring Real-World Fashion

The impact of virtual fashion in music videos extends beyond the virtual realm. The avant-garde and futuristic designs showcased in music videos often inspire real-world fashion trends. Fashion enthusiasts and designers draw inspiration from these virtual fashion creations and incorporate elements of virtual fashion into their own designs. This cross-pollination between virtual and physical fashion creates a dynamic and ever-evolving fashion landscape.

7.4.9 The Future of Virtual Fashion in Music Videos

As technology continues to advance, the future of virtual fashion in music videos looks promising. With the rise of virtual reality and augmented reality, artists will have even more tools at their disposal to create immersive and interactive fashion experiences. Virtual fashion will continue to evolve, blurring the lines between the virtual and physical worlds, and revolutionizing the way we perceive fashion and music.

In conclusion, virtual fashion has become an integral part of music videos, allowing artists to create unique visual identities, enhance the visual experience, and push the boundaries of creativity. Collaborations between artists and virtual fashion designers have resulted in groundbreaking fashion concepts that inspire real-world fashion trends. As technology advances, the future of virtual fashion in music videos holds endless possibilities for creating immersive and interactive fashion experiences.

8 Preparing for the Future of Virtual Fashion

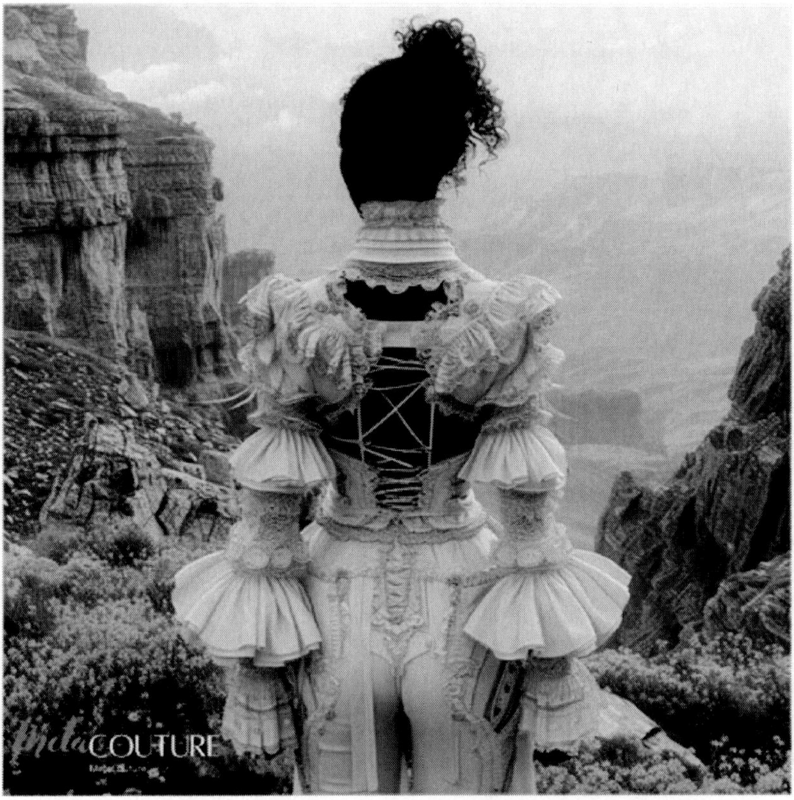

8.1 Skills and Education for Virtual Fashion Designers

As the fashion industry continues to evolve, virtual fashion design is becoming an increasingly important field. Designing couture fashion for avatars requires a unique set of skills and knowledge that traditional fashion designers may not possess. In this section, we will explore the skills and education needed to excel in the world of virtual fashion design.

8.1.1 Understanding Virtual Fashion Design

Before delving into the specific skills required for virtual fashion design, it is essential to have a solid understanding of the field. Virtual fashion design involves creating digital garments and accessories for virtual avatars. It combines elements of traditional fashion design with technology, such as 3D modeling, simulation, and rendering.

To excel in virtual fashion design, it is crucial to have a strong foundation in traditional fashion design principles. Understanding garment construction, fabric selection, and fashion trends will provide a solid base for creating virtual couture.

8.1.2 Proficiency in 3D Modeling and Simulation

One of the key skills for virtual fashion designers is proficiency in 3D modeling and simulation software. These tools allow designers to create realistic virtual garments and visualize how they will drape and move on avatars. Learning software such as CLO 3D, Marvelous Designer, or Browzwear will be invaluable in creating accurate virtual couture.

Understanding the principles of 3D modeling, such as creating and manipulating digital patterns, will enable designers to bring their virtual garments to life. Additionally, knowledge of simulation techniques, such as fabric physics and garment simulation, will ensure that the virtual couture behaves realistically.

8.1.3 Technical Knowledge of Virtual Reality and Augmented Reality

Virtual fashion designers should also have a solid understanding of virtual reality (VR) and augmented reality (AR) technologies. VR allows users to immerse themselves in a virtual environment, while AR overlays digital elements onto the real world. Both technologies have the potential to revolutionize the way we experience fashion.

By understanding the capabilities and limitations of VR and AR, designers can create virtual fashion experiences that are both visually stunning and user-friendly. They can design garments that interact with the virtual environment or incorporate AR elements into their designs. Knowledge of VR and AR platforms, such as Oculus Rift or Microsoft HoloLens, will be beneficial in creating cutting-edge virtual fashion.

8.1.4 Creativity and Innovation

While technical skills are essential, creativity and innovation are equally important in virtual fashion design. Virtual fashion designers must push the boundaries of what is possible and create unique and captivating designs for avatars. They should be able to think outside the box and experiment with new materials, shapes, and textures.

Innovation in virtual fashion design can also extend to sustainability and ethical considerations. Designers can explore ways to reduce the environmental impact of virtual fashion or incorporate ethical practices into their virtual couture. By combining creativity with a forward-thinking mindset, virtual fashion designers can shape the future of the industry.

8.1.5 Collaboration and Communication

Virtual fashion design often involves collaboration with other professionals, such as 3D modelers, animators, and programmers. Therefore, strong collaboration and communication skills are crucial for success in this field. Designers must be able to effectively communicate their vision and work collaboratively to bring it to life.

Collaboration also extends to working with clients and understanding their needs and preferences. Virtual fashion designers should be able to interpret client briefs and translate them into virtual couture that meets their expectations. Building strong relationships with clients and colleagues will be essential for a successful career in virtual fashion design.

8.1.6 Continuous Learning and Adaptability

The field of virtual fashion design is constantly evolving, with new technologies and techniques emerging regularly. Therefore, virtual fashion designers must have a mindset of continuous learning and adaptability. Staying up to date with the latest advancements in 3D modeling, simulation, and virtual reality will ensure that designers remain at the forefront of the industry.

Attending workshops, conferences, and online courses focused on virtual fashion design can provide valuable insights and opportunities for skill development. Additionally, experimenting with new software and techniques will help designers stay innovative and adaptable in an ever-changing industry.

8.1.7 Education and Training

While there is no specific degree or certification required to become a virtual fashion designer, formal education in fashion design or a related field can provide a solid foundation. Many universities and design schools now offer courses or specializations in virtual fashion design, which can provide valuable knowledge and practical experience.

In addition to formal education, self-learning through online tutorials, forums, and communities can also be beneficial. Building a portfolio of virtual fashion designs and participating in virtual fashion design competitions can showcase skills and attract potential clients or employers.

8.1.8 Conclusion

Virtual fashion design is an exciting and rapidly growing field that offers endless possibilities for creativity and innovation. To excel in this field, virtual fashion designers need a combination of technical skills, creativity, collaboration, and adaptability. By continuously learning and staying at the forefront of technology, designers can shape the future of virtual fashion and create stunning couture for avatars.

8.2 Collaboration in Virtual Fashion Design

Collaboration is a crucial aspect of any creative industry, and virtual fashion design is no exception. In the rapidly evolving world of virtual fashion, designers need to work together with various professionals to bring their visions to life. Collaboration not only enhances the quality of the final product but also opens up new possibilities and pushes the boundaries of virtual fashion design. In this section, we will explore the importance of collaboration in virtual fashion design and how designers can prepare for it.

8.2.1 Collaborating with Virtual Fashion Technologists

Virtual fashion design requires a deep understanding of technology and its integration with fashion. To create stunning virtual couture, designers need to collaborate with virtual fashion technologists who specialize in the technical aspects of virtual fashion. These technologists have expertise in areas such as virtual reality, augmented reality, 3D modeling, and simulation. By working together, designers and technologists can leverage their respective skills to create immersive and realistic virtual fashion experiences.

Collaboration with virtual fashion technologists also enables designers to stay updated with the latest technological advancements. As technology continues to evolve, new tools and techniques emerge that can enhance the virtual fashion design process. By collaborating with technologists, designers can gain insights into these advancements and incorporate them into their designs, pushing the boundaries of virtual fashion even further.

8.2.2 Collaboration with Virtual Fabric Experts

Fabric plays a vital role in fashion design, and the same holds true for virtual fashion. Collaborating with virtual fabric experts can help designers select the most suitable virtual fabrics for their couture creations. These experts have in-depth knowledge of virtual fabric properties, textures, and draping behavior. By working closely with them, designers can ensure that their virtual garments look and feel realistic.

Virtual fabric experts can also assist designers in adapting real-world fabric designs for virtual use. They can provide guidance on how to translate intricate fabric patterns and textures into the virtual environment. Collaboration with these experts allows designers to explore a wide range of virtual fabric options and experiment with innovative designs that may not be possible in the physical world.

8.2.3 Collaboration with Virtual Fashion Marketers

In the digital age, marketing plays a crucial role in the success of any fashion brand, including virtual fashion. Collaborating with virtual fashion marketers can help designers effectively promote their virtual couture collections and reach a wider audience. These marketers specialize in leveraging social media, influencer marketing, and virtual fashion advertising to create buzz around virtual fashion brands.

By collaborating with virtual fashion marketers, designers can gain valuable insights into the preferences and behaviors of the target audience. This knowledge can inform the design process, ensuring that the virtual couture collections resonate with the intended audience. Additionally, marketers can provide guidance on branding, positioning, and pricing strategies, helping designers create a strong and compelling virtual fashion brand.

8.2.4 Collaboration with Other Virtual Fashion Designers

Collaboration among virtual fashion designers is essential for fostering creativity and innovation in the industry. By working together, designers can share ideas, exchange feedback, and inspire each other to push the boundaries of virtual fashion design. Collaborative platforms and communities provide a space for designers to connect, collaborate, and showcase their work.

Collaborating with other designers also opens up opportunities for joint projects and collaborations. Designers can come together to create virtual fashion collections, organize virtual fashion shows, or collaborate on virtual fashion campaigns. These collaborations not only enhance the quality of the final product but also create a sense of community and camaraderie among virtual fashion designers.

8.2.5 Preparing for Collaboration in Virtual Fashion Design

To prepare for collaboration in virtual fashion design, designers should focus on developing certain skills and adopting a collaborative mindset. Here are some key steps to consider:

1. **Continuous Learning:** Stay updated with the latest advancements in virtual fashion technology, fabric simulation, and marketing strategies. Attend workshops,

conferences, and online courses to enhance your knowledge and skills.

2. **Networking:** Build a strong network of professionals in the virtual fashion industry, including technologists, fabric experts, marketers, and other designers. Attend industry events, join virtual fashion communities, and engage in online forums to connect with like-minded individuals.
3. **Effective Communication:** Develop strong communication skills to effectively convey your ideas and collaborate with others. Clear and concise communication is essential for successful collaboration in virtual fashion design.
4. **Open-mindedness:** Embrace new ideas and perspectives. Collaboration often involves compromise and the blending of different creative visions. Be open to exploring new possibilities and incorporating feedback from collaborators.
5. **Adaptability:** Virtual fashion is a rapidly evolving field, and designers need to be adaptable to keep up with the changes. Embrace new technologies, techniques, and trends, and be willing to experiment and take risks in your designs.

By embracing collaboration and preparing for it, virtual fashion designers can unlock new creative possibilities and shape the future of the industry. Collaboration not only enhances the quality of virtual fashion designs but also fosters innovation and pushes the boundaries of what is possible in the virtual fashion world.

8.3 The Future of Virtual Fashion Industry

As technology continues to advance at an unprecedented rate, the future of the virtual fashion industry holds immense potential. The possibilities for designing couture fashion for avatars are endless, and it is crucial for fashion designers to stay ahead of the curve and prepare themselves for the exciting developments that lie ahead.

8.3.1 Virtual Reality Integration

One of the most significant advancements in the future of virtual fashion is the integration of virtual reality (VR) technology. VR allows users to immerse themselves in a completely digital environment, providing a unique and interactive experience. In the context of fashion, VR can revolutionize the way designers create and showcase their collections.

With VR, designers can create virtual showrooms where users can explore and interact with their designs in a three-dimensional space. This technology enables fashion enthusiasts to experience the garments in a more immersive and realistic way, as if they were physically present at a fashion show. Designers can also use VR to collaborate with other professionals in real-time, regardless of their physical location, making the design process more efficient and inclusive.

8.3.2 Artificial Intelligence and Machine Learning

Artificial intelligence (AI) and machine learning (ML) are rapidly transforming various industries, and the virtual fashion industry is no exception. These technologies have the potential to revolutionize the way avatars are created and customized, making them more realistic and personalized.

AI algorithms can analyze vast amounts of data to understand individual preferences, body measurements, and style choices. This information can then be used to generate avatars that accurately represent the user's unique characteristics and fashion preferences. Machine learning algorithms can also continuously learn and adapt to user feedback, ensuring that the avatars evolve and improve over time.

Furthermore, AI and ML can assist designers in the creation process by generating design suggestions based on user preferences and current fashion trends. This technology can help streamline the design process and provide designers with valuable insights and inspiration.

8.3.3 Virtual Fabric Innovation

In the future, virtual fashion designers will have access to a wide range of innovative virtual fabrics. These fabrics will not only mimic the look and feel of real textiles but also possess unique properties that are impossible to achieve with traditional materials.

Virtual fabrics can be designed to change color, texture, and pattern with a simple command, allowing users to customize their garments according to their preferences. Additionally, these fabrics can be programmed to respond to environmental factors such as temperature and humidity, providing a dynamic and interactive fashion experience.

The development of virtual fabrics also presents an opportunity for sustainable fashion practices. Virtual fabrics do not require the use of physical resources, reducing waste and environmental impact. Designers can experiment with different materials and textures without the need for physical prototypes, further minimizing their carbon footprint.

8.3.4 Virtual Fashion Communities and Social Platforms

In the future, virtual fashion communities and social platforms will play a crucial role in the industry. These platforms will provide a space for fashion enthusiasts, designers, and brands to connect, collaborate, and showcase their creations.

Virtual fashion communities will allow users to share their designs, receive feedback, and participate in virtual fashion competitions. These platforms will foster creativity and innovation, enabling designers to gain recognition and build a following.

Social platforms will also serve as a powerful marketing tool for virtual fashion brands. Influencers and trendsetters in the virtual fashion industry will emerge, shaping the tastes and preferences of the community. Brands will need to adapt their marketing strategies to effectively engage with this new generation of influencers and consumers.

8.3.5 Sustainability and Ethical Considerations

As the virtual fashion industry continues to grow, sustainability and ethical considerations will become increasingly important. Designers will need to prioritize sustainable practices in the creation and production of virtual garments.

Virtual fashion offers the opportunity to reduce waste and minimize the environmental impact associated with traditional fashion. By embracing virtual fashion, designers can contribute to a more sustainable future by reducing the consumption of physical resources and minimizing carbon emissions.

Ethical considerations will also come into play as virtual fashion becomes more prevalent. Designers will need to ensure that the virtual garments they create do not perpetuate harmful stereotypes or cultural appropriation. It will be essential to promote diversity, inclusivity, and ethical practices within the virtual fashion industry.

8.3.6 Continuous Learning and Adaptation

To thrive in the future of virtual fashion, designers must embrace a mindset of continuous learning and adaptation. The industry is evolving rapidly, and staying up-to-date with the latest technologies and trends will be crucial.

Designers should invest in their education and acquire the necessary skills to navigate the virtual fashion landscape. This may involve learning new software, understanding virtual reality technologies, and staying informed about advancements in AI and ML.

Collaboration with other professionals in the field will also be essential. By working together, designers can share knowledge, exchange ideas, and push the boundaries of virtual fashion design.

8.3.7 Conclusion

The future of the virtual fashion industry is bright and full of possibilities. With advancements in technology, designers can create couture fashion for avatars that is immersive, personalized, and sustainable. By embracing virtual reality, artificial intelligence, and virtual fabrics, designers can revolutionize the way fashion is created, showcased, and experienced. It is crucial for designers to prepare themselves for this future by continuously learning, collaborating, and embracing the exciting opportunities that lie ahead.

8.4 Embracing Virtual Fashion as a Designer

As the fashion industry continues to evolve, virtual fashion has emerged as a powerful and innovative medium for designers to express their creativity. With the rise of virtual reality and augmented reality technologies, the possibilities for designing couture fashion for avatars are endless. In this section, we will explore how designers can embrace virtual fashion and prepare for the future of this exciting industry.

8.4.1 Understanding the Potential of Virtual Fashion

Virtual fashion offers designers a unique opportunity to push the boundaries of creativity and explore new design concepts. By designing for avatars, designers can experiment with unconventional shapes, materials, and textures that may not be feasible in the physical world. Virtual fashion allows for the creation of garments that defy gravity, change color with a touch, or transform into entirely new designs with a simple command.

Designers can also leverage the interactive nature of virtual fashion to create immersive experiences for their audience. By incorporating motion sensors and haptic feedback, designers can bring their garments to life, allowing users to interact with and experience the designs in a whole new way. Virtual fashion opens up a world of possibilities for designers to create truly unique and unforgettable fashion experiences.

8.4.2 Mastering Virtual Fashion Tools and Technologies

To fully embrace virtual fashion, designers need to familiarize themselves with the tools and technologies that enable its creation. This includes learning 3D modeling and simulation software, virtual reality and augmented reality platforms, and virtual fashion rendering techniques. By mastering these tools, designers can bring their virtual designs to life and showcase them in a realistic and visually stunning manner.

Additionally, designers should stay up-to-date with the latest advancements in virtual fashion technology. As the industry continues to evolve, new tools and technologies will emerge, offering designers even more possibilities for creativity. By staying informed and continuously learning, designers can stay ahead of the curve and take full advantage of the opportunities presented by virtual fashion.

8.4.3 Collaborating with Virtual Fashion Experts

Collaboration is key in the world of virtual fashion. Designers should seek out partnerships with experts in virtual fashion technology, such as 3D modelers, animators, and programmers. By working together, designers can leverage the expertise of these professionals to bring their virtual designs to life in the most realistic and engaging way possible.

Furthermore, collaboration extends beyond the virtual realm. Designers should also collaborate with other fashion professionals, such as stylists, photographers, and makeup artists, to create a cohesive and impactful virtual fashion experience. By combining their skills and expertise, designers can create virtual fashion campaigns and shows that rival their physical counterparts.

8.4.4 Experimenting with Virtual Fabrication Techniques

Virtual fashion opens up new possibilities for fabricating garments. Designers can experiment with virtual fabric simulation, allowing them to test different materials and textures without the need for physical prototypes. This not only saves time and resources but also enables designers to explore unconventional materials that may not be readily available in the physical world.

Additionally, designers can explore sustainable virtual fabrication techniques. By using virtual materials that mimic the properties of real fabrics, designers can reduce waste and minimize the environmental impact of their designs. Virtual fashion also allows for easy customization and personalization, enabling designers to create made-to-order garments that fit perfectly without the need for extensive alterations.

8.4.5 Embracing Virtual Fashion as a Sustainable Alternative

Virtual fashion has the potential to revolutionize the industry by offering a sustainable alternative to traditional fashion practices. By embracing virtual fashion, designers can reduce the environmental impact of their designs by minimizing waste, energy consumption, and carbon emissions associated with physical garment production.

Furthermore, virtual fashion allows for a more inclusive and diverse representation of beauty. Designers can create avatars that represent a wide range of body types, ethnicities, and identities, challenging the narrow beauty standards often perpetuated in the physical fashion industry. Virtual fashion has the power to celebrate individuality and promote inclusivity, making fashion accessible to all.

8.4.6 Navigating the Future of Virtual Fashion

As virtual fashion continues to evolve, designers must be adaptable and open to change. The future of virtual fashion holds endless possibilities, from advancements in virtual reality technology to the integration of artificial intelligence in the design process. Designers should embrace these changes and be willing to experiment with new ideas and techniques.

Additionally, designers should stay connected with the virtual fashion community. Attending virtual fashion conferences, participating in online forums, and networking with other virtual fashion enthusiasts can provide valuable insights and opportunities for collaboration. By staying engaged and connected, designers can stay at the forefront of the virtual fashion industry and continue to push the boundaries of creativity.

In conclusion, embracing virtual fashion as a designer requires a willingness to explore new technologies, collaborate with experts, and experiment with innovative fabrication techniques. By understanding the potential of virtual fashion, mastering the necessary tools and technologies, and embracing sustainability and inclusivity, designers can prepare themselves for the future of this exciting industry. Virtual fashion offers endless possibilities for creativity and innovation, and by embracing it, designers can shape the future of fashion in a truly transformative way.